Steps to Yoga

With kind regards, ॐ and prem

Swami Niranjan

Steps to Yoga

&

Yoga Initiation Papers

(Letters to Vishwaprem and Satyabrat)

Swami Satyananda Saraswati

Yoga Publications Trust, Munger, Bihar, India

Published by Bihar School of Yoga
    Reprinted 1984

Published by Yoga Publications Trust
    Reprinted 2005

ISBN: 81-85787-13-1

Publisher and distributor: Yoga Publications Trust, Ganga Darshan, Munger, Bihar, India.

Website: www.yogavision.net

Printed at Thomson Press (India) Limited, New Delhi, 110001

SWAMI SIVANANDA SARASWATI

Swami Sivananda was born at Patta-madai, Tamil Nadu, in 1887. After serving as a medical doctor in Malaya, he renounced his practice, went to Rishikesh and was initiated into Dashnami sannyasa in 1924 by Swami Vishwananda Saraswati. He toured extensively throughout India, inspiring people to practise yoga and lead a divine life. He founded the Divine Life Society at Rishikesh in 1936, the Sivananda Ayurvedic Pharmacy in 1945, the Yoga Vedanta Forest Academy in 1948 and the Sivananda Eye Hospital in 1957. During his lifetime Swami Sivananda guided thousands of disciples and aspirants all over the world and authored over 200 books.

SWAMI SATYANANDA SARASWATI

Swami Satyananda was born at Almora, Uttar Pradesh, in 1923. In 1943 he met Swami Sivananda in Rishikesh and adopted the Dashnami sannyasa way of life. In 1955 he left his guru's ashram to live as a wandering mendicant and later founded the International Yoga Fellowship in 1956 and the Bihar School of Yoga in 1963. Over the next 20 years Swami Satyananda toured internationally and authored over 80 books. In 1987 he founded Sivananda Math, a charitable institution for aiding rural development, and the Yoga Research Foundation. In 1988 he renounced his mission, adopting kshetra sannyasa, and now lives as a paramahamsa sannyasin.

SWAMI NIRANJANANANDA SARASWATI

Swami Niranjanananda was born in Madhya Pradesh in 1960. At the age of four he joined the Bihar School of Yoga and was initiated into Dashnami sannyasa at the age of ten. From 1971 he travelled overseas and toured many countries for the next 11 years. In 1983 he was recalled to India and appointed President of Bihar School of Yoga. Since then he has guided the development of Ganga Darshan, Sivananda Math, Yoga Publications Trust and the Yoga Research Foundation. In 1990 he was initiated as a paramahamsa and in 1993 anointed preceptor in succession to Swami Satyananda. Bihar Yoga Bharati was founded under his direction in 1994. He has authored over 20 books and guides national and international yoga programs.

SWAMI SATYASANGANANDA SARASWATI

Swami Satyasangananda (Satsangi) was born on 24th March 1953, in Chandorenagore, West Bengal. From the age of 22 she experienced a series of inner awakenings which led her to her guru, Swami Satyananda. From 1981 she travelled ceaselessly with her guru in India and overseas and developed into a scholar with deep insight into the yogic and tantric traditions as well as modern sciences and philosophies. She is an efficient channel for the transmission of her guru's teachings. The establishment of Sivananda Math in Rikhia is her creation and mission, and she guides all its activities there, working tirelessly to uplift the weaker and underprivileged areas. She embodies compassion with clear reason and is the foundation of her guru's vision.

Contents

Contents

Listen! O virtuous ones! Listen!
O intelligent ones! Listen to the clarion call of the
countless siddhas:

"No sooner is the ego surrendered than the Divine Master is revealed; the Dark Night of the Soul is transformed into illumined awareness."

Guru Gorakhnath

शान्ति पाठ
SHANTI PATH

ॐ सहनाववतु । सह नौ भुनक्तु । सह वीर्यं करवावहै । तेजस्वि नावधीतमस्तु ।
मा विद्विषावहै ॥

ॐ शान्ति: शान्ति: शान्ति:

Aum Saha Naavavatu; Saha Nau Bhunaktu;. Saha Veeryam
Karavaavahai; Tejasvi Naavadheetamastu; Maa Vidvishaavahai.

Aum Shaantih Shaantih Shaantih

Aum. May the Lord protect both teacher and disciple, and
may He cherish us both. May we work with full energy, that
our study be perfect and give good results. May we never
feel ill will towards each other.

Aum peace, peace, peace

Introduction

This book is compiled from a series of letters written by Swami Satyananda to two of his disciples, guiding them through their sadhana and awakening. He is speaking to them from a higher level of consciousness in a manner appropriate to their individual understanding and sadhana, and not speaking with mundane awareness, or in the form of a text.

In order to go through the process of awakening, it is necessary for a person to become a disciple and experience the guru from a state which is beyond the intelligent mind, creating an intimate rapport with him and finding no distinction between a master, a philosopher, a friend, a relative and God.

This book is for those who are seekers wanting invaluable guidance to take them on the path of realization and inner awakening by harmoniously reconciling the philosophy of yoga with its practice.

Letters to Vishwaprem

Do you believe in God? Is he kind? Do you feel it? Should I tell an eternal truth?

He is mysterious. Mysterious are his ways. He rendered him debauched first – only to make him an immortal saint for millions – a Surdas!

He sent Gautam Buddha to the forest just to make him wise enough to preach that it was not necessary for nirvana. Infinitely gracious is he. Will you believe?

There is no other way, except letting him do his choice.

There is no alternative to his un-understandable lila.

And he went to influence Kaikeyi. He went into exile for fourteen years. What for? We finite mortals don't know and can't know his infinite blessings in disguise.

Pain is a cross onto which nature hangs a man whenever she wishes to make him a sublime superman.

Bliss is your birthright, not sorrow. Freedom is thy heritage, not bondage.

And so when we are exhausted, let us offer everything unto him. Let him do the rest because he knows. Let us stop, for we know not.

Ye hypocrite! Ye Bahoorupiye! Self-conceited man, better say "No God" than falsely pretending bhakti. You are an outright atheist. You want *your* will to come true. You don't want *his* will to prevail.

So come to his sharan, his refuge, and surrender yourself unto Him.

Sivanandnagar, March 13, 1956

In order to develop love for God in your heart, express love through service of and sympathy for mankind. See God in them; they are conscious forms of God or chalta phirta Rama.

Consider yourself very near to God. He is in the idol also.

God likes smiles and joy. You too must remain ever cheerful. In spite of the fact that you have material things available to you, your mind sometimes remains dull, depressed and dissatisfied. Why? You yourself do not know the reason.

Keep your body and mind always busy in some work. Work purifies the soul. After mental purification you will attain spontaneous success in meditation. Mukti is impossible without karma yoga. Perfect happiness is experienced only after one has introspected and analyzed oneself and then taken to the path of sadhana and thus determined to lead a virtuous and divine life.

Instead of being led away by emotions, you will have to control them. External as well as internal sadhanas are essential for this. Your life will be moulded properly by virtue of the company of saints and satsang. However, satsang for one hour or half an hour alone will not do you any remarkable good. It is only when we live with saints for some time that we are impressed by their realizations, life and other virtues.

Rishikesh, March 25, 1956

Keep a spiritual diary every day. This will be most helpful for your own self-reflection and also I can follow your daily progress.

Get up at 4 or 5 a.m. Do japa, dhyana and asana; then go to your office. Fulfil the office duties with cheerfulness, peace, love, inspiration and selflessness. Again at night do japa, kirtan and satsang. Think over how you passed the whole day and try to make better resolves. These are the fundamental principles of keeping a diary.

Doubts do arise in every mind. Why did God make this world? What is the use of yogic sadhana when even a leaf can't move without his orders? If everybody is God, what is good or bad then? All these doubts are such that we have no concern with them. We can lead a peaceful and happy life even without

4

thinking all this. If there is transmigration or not, how are we concerned? We have just to throw impurities out of ourselves. We have to sublimate lower impulses into higher missions. We have to fill ourselves with divine virtues. We have to keep our family, neighbours, relatives and friends happy.

So, my child, try to make your life eternally divine through the process of sadhana. Whenever you get some time, do go to satsangs and gradually learn the art of assimilating the gifts of satsang. Encourage your friends and neighbours to tread the path of truth and lead a divine life. Do read yogic and vedantic literature and reflect over what you have read. Do surya namaskara. Don't worry about your eyesight. It is enough to have the eye of intuition.

I am sure you will walk on the path of spiritual sadhana and lead a divine life. Infinite blessings for your success.

Never think of renouncing your home and avocation and going anywhere, even if anyone tells you a million times. Thy house is a tirtha, thy body is a mandir, thy soul is thy devata and thou art his pujarin.

I am sure that you must be carrying on your sadhana enthusiastically. There is no noise in the world; there is no peace in the Himalayas! Both are within you. You can have darshan of God if you can make your mind desireless. It is impossible to have his darshan even in the Himalayas if you don't have faith in God and practical interest in sadhana. Therefore, the essential thing is to correct the mind and keep on removing unnecessary thoughts. While it is true, my child, that one can have darshan of God even at home, it is also a fact that one can find peace in the world as well.

Renunciation of society or sannyasa is not as important for spiritual life as brahmacharya, service, dhyana and asanas. Start sadhana at 4 a.m. daily. Practise yogasanas for 10–15 minutes after answering the calls of nature and taking a wash or a bath. Then do japa and practise meditation on your Ishta. Japa and meditation may be practised at night also before going to bed. Besides all these, realize that the domestic work and studies are also Ishwara sadhanas provided they are done with full concentration, love, inspiration and with the bhava of his worship.

I am confident that you will put into practice what Satyam has hitherto told you. Let me know your progress by sending your spiritual diary to me once every month.

Always remember that the world is full of selfishness! You should think twice or even more before putting a step forward. You must have the strength to stand on your own feet. Every moment of your life must be dedicated to higher ideals. Equip yourself with good speech, good health and sound education. Thus you will be able to serve people in a better way. I am ready to guide you.

Don't think of renouncing. I don't approve of your miscalculation. Let me know that you have accepted my rulings.

Bhagalpur (Bihar), April 20, 1957

I am very happy to survey your program. Life must go on like this. You should not allow the mind to sit idle even for a minute. The first step to spiritual life is to keep the mind ever busy. Every work is sadhana if done with concentration. The worship of God and offering of flowers go to waste if the mind of the sadhaka is caught in the net of desires and passions. Become the master of your mind by applying it to various jobs from morning till night. Do your work efficiently and with full concentration. Office work is also bhagavad aradhana provided the mind is made free from all desires.

It is absolutely necessary for you to have one aim in life. You can easily succeed in accomplishing even great works if only you have a dhun. I have great hopes that you will prepare yourself and make yourself fit enough to serve humanity. Blessed will be your life if you do something good in this life. Gather your powers. Keep your life pure and noble. Render your thoughts spiritual. It is unworthy for sadhakas to be led astray in this world of passions and temptations. Diligent sadhakas always live aloof from artificial

6

and impure thoughts. Why? Because they want to offer their life as a flower unto the lotus feet of the beloved Lord with all its freshness, beauty and unsmelt fragrance.

Your program of sadhana is very inspiring. Don't merely write items of your external life in your diary. Your diary should be a record of your experiences and thoughts and emotions, a copy of which you should always keep with you. It will be a fine garland of your thoughts. On surveying your monthly report of spiritual sadhana, it seems to me that your mind hardly gets any time to think rubbish and wander aimlessly. Let your mind remain tied up with the strings of action even as at present. This is the way towards spiritual progress.

Yes, do read the Gita whenever you get time. But, my child, this life itself is a never-ending Gita. One can learn so many wonderful things from this living Gita. This living Gita is wonderful. I have read this life-Gita. May you also try to understand at least the first word of this life-Gita, and put the same into practice.

Delhi, May 1, 1957

Do regular asanas for a little more time. Do them for up to half an hour. You need not do yoga sadhana for hours. If you understand the real thing, your mind will merge as soon as you sit for meditation in padmasana.

Repeat his name at all times. Don't meditate in the office. Of course, you can reflect over the 'faith culture'. Whenever you find leisure time you can either read your diary or repeat the mantra mentally. If you meditate on your way to or in the office, you will become absent-minded. I don't want you to land yourself on the plane of emotional awakening or meditational contemplation during office hours. You will be able to see him in meditation, even if you devote ten to twelve hours to extroversion. The fact is that even one hour of introversion can result in samadhi provided one is sincere and true in one's practices of meditation.

7

Likewise, don't practise meditation while doing asanas. Do nama smaran. Adjust your sadhana. Use common sense. There should be no hard and fast rule while doing sadhana. Repeat the mantra mentally while performing asanas.

Don't grow impatient if you find it difficult to bring the form before your mental eyes. It takes time. Time depends upon the fulfilment of sense withdrawal. Withdrawal of the senses depends solely upon love, sincerity and one-pointed faith in your ideal. Since you have all the accessories for sense withdrawal (love, sincerity and one-pointed faith), you will see him through your mental eyes, irrespective of time, space and objective factors. Conflicts, struggles, worries, anxieties and passions should be calmed down by the virtues of love, sincerity and faith. Be unruffled; be detached from all mental charges of good and bad.

Spare a few minutes for atma chintan in your diary. It should be something like intuitional flashes, not simply emotional poetry. Emotionalism is also necessary, I don't deny it, but it should be backed by intuition.

Delhi, May 7, 1957

You are a hard and sincere worker; I don't doubt your success. I expect of you similar hard and sincere work throughout your life. This is the eternal path upon which you have to walk. I don't want to see you idle, luxurious, self-contented, complacent and a lover of the happy-go-lucky life like many children in society. I want to see you ever progressive, merged in hard work, full of divine virtues and a helper of mankind. Millions of girls are thinking 'something' in one or the other corner of the world. If you also enrol your name in that list, where then is the novelty?

Express your emotions in the 'Ganga of Thoughts'. Write down your thoughts both in Hindi and English. Great is your aim; grander still are your efforts; noblest of all is your soul. You are not born just to live and die. You have a

8

great mission to fulfil, for which every step of your life is a mighty system of 'preparation'.

Your address 'Beloved Father' is better and more apt then 'Revered Master'. Do address me as such. Do accept this relationship also. May the Almighty Lord give you more strength to fulfil the great task which lies ahead of you!

Raipur (Rewa), August 2, 1957

Education is quite essential nowadays. People of your sex need it very much in order to be able to lead an independent life. It is very risky for girls to remain in ashrams. They need to have an independent career at all costs. Education provides them with sufficient means to live without being obligated to anybody. In order to realize God one need not join any ashram, nor need one wander hither and thither. What exactly one needs is a guide; that is all. Further, one should strive under the guidance of his master.

So study hard and get yourself educated academically. Side by side keep the light of yoga alive in every atom of your being. It is enough at present if you keep your mind engaged in hard work. Enough it is if you lead a regular, pure and hard-working life for the present.

In addition to this, do your bit of sadhana whenever you have spare time. Work purifies the soul. Then the inner light begins to unfold itself.

Instead of thinking and brooding, please go on working and remembering his name. The whole world is your friend. You need not sit alone and feel lonely and brood over and over again. Your future has been decided. Education, sadhana, service of mankind. Do shake off your heart, brush up your willpower and strongly resolve:

1. I will get myself educated.
2. I will remember God at all times.
3. I will serve all in my available capacities.
4. I will live a life of intense purity in thought, word and deed.

9

Daydreams are always golden, but they don't come true. On the other hand, they nourish disappointments, cause pain and neurosis. As a promising sadhaka you must be careful of such dreams.

Do not be diffident. Your self is noble and great. You inherit truth and purity. You have in you infinite capacities. You just have to assert what you are. I conduct prayers for you. May you be able to achieve your goal of shanti and shakti, peace and strength.

Please put up substantially hard work. Waste not a single moment in laziness, brooding, dreaming, worrying and weeping. Become an incarnation of joy and happiness. Lead a proper life while adjusting yourself with the family environment. Always remember that you have a noble mission for which you are working and getting ready.

Mathura, September 21, 1957

Don't think of rest, 'rest' is 'rust'. Nothing else but rust. Work does purify the soul; you are quite right in thinking thus. Never get excited about your office job. Keep a cool head and a balanced mind. Excitement brings about depression and consequently terrible fatigue. "Balance of mind and efficiency in one's duties is yoga."

Always be happy and cheerful. Life is true. Life is a joy. Cast off all mental and physical burdens. Sorrows and gloom of the mind should become unto thee like a range of passing clouds in windy winter, only to be scattered after a while. Nothing should destroy the peace of your mind. For nothing in the world should you barter the joy of your soul. You must become an incarnation of perceptible smiles and imperceptible shanti.

There are numerous unlucky events in the life of everyone, which suppress the joy of the soul and throw you into gloom. Do understand this and keep on brushing your soul free of all gloomy impressions of day to day life.

God's awards are not according to the worth of man, but according to his own ever kindliness. So one need not be perplexed by the conceptions of sin and so on. Sin and infidelity are far from one who knows the inner ruler.

Marching thus upon the road of eternal life, don't look back at your past; don't look too far. Instead keep your vision at a little distance, a little ahead of the present. This is how you will complete the journey of your life.

Rajnandgaon, January 17, 1958

This world is a school wherein we learn so many lessons provided we are keen and alert. There is nothing permanent here where one can rest. Thy soul is eternal. You should rest there. In this temporary world one has to work hard. Hard work purifies the soul.

God is merciful. He knows what is good for you. You should never lose heart. Don't be puffed up by success; never be disappointed by momentary failures.

Worldly people are sweet in speech. They are terribly bitter in nature. So don't be deluded and hypnotized by lavish praise and buttering up. Remember you are born for a higher purpose; the present stage is just a phase of preparation. The moment you are ready for that higher mission, you will be initiated into a still greater order. Until then work in the office, study your lessons, sublimate your emotions, clear up the dirt of your personality, work hard in the turmoil of city life, enrich your experience and strengthen your soul.

I have accepted you as my shishya and I expect of you a good deal of spiritual firmness. I don't want you to be a weeping machine, a stock of emotions, a bundle of lower instincts, a symbol of melancholy and sadness. Don't hate the world; learn from it the glory of the Divine Father – his wonderful lilas!

You have pledged to realize your real divine nature. This sankalpa will help you in sadhana. I am ever ready to come

11

to you in dhyana; but for the present, telepathic communications appear like dreams. There does not seem to be any chance of our supra-sensual communication at present. But I am sure that your intensified will and receptivity will mobilize your scheme, will create opportunities and possibilities so as to enable me to give you a complete revelation.

How are you to prepare yourself for this great event? Please, attention! Be regular in japa, kirtan and meditation. Stop crying, control emotional breakdowns.

I am sending you 'Yoga Initiation Papers' by separate post. Please study these initiation papers from time to time and put the instructions into practice.

Rajnandgaon, January 22, 1958

You have decided your mission finally. You may starve, you may suffer; yet you will have to move on and on. Nothing earthly or heavenly should take you from the path. You must be divine; that is all.

I am in tune with you every day between 5.30 and 6 a.m.

Be careful about your health. You have to do a good lot of work. Don't think that the present work is an obstacle. You have to live in the world. Continue the work as usual. *Change is always internal!* Please be quick and efficient in your office work. Don't change your views about office work even if you have to renounce it, say, after a few years. Even at the time of renouncing you should have no low opinion about the same, otherwise that would become one of your great spiritual disqualifications.

Your bhakti should be expressed in three ways: (a) success in sadhana, (b) normal work and also (c) further studies. Don't feel tired. It is always good to practise concentration regularly and punctually. Don't overdo it. Dharana should come by itself. Love should bring about spontaneous success. Please write letters only pertaining to your sadhana and

12

experiences, mental poise and disturbances, so that I may guide you. I must prepare you at once. I must sublimate your emotions into mysticism, meditation and samadhi. Your letters should be a sort of description of your meditation, an essay, so to say.

Yes, you are Gaya and Kashi. You have no other place for pilgrimage except your own atma. You will awaken all tirthas within yourself when you have realized that atma.

Rajnandgaon, January 27, 1958

Do not think of thought communication at present. Every mystic art will automatically be revealed unto you even without your knowledge – not to talk of efforts – at an opportune moment.

Do not at all miss sight of your goal, i.e. the realization of conscious form. Unless this consciousness manifests, there is no use worrying about thought communication. Did I not tell you that your inner consciousness is always plugged into my form, ideas, etc. through the channel of awareness? Since your self-consciousness has not been able to peep inside, the form and ideas do not manifest in your conscious region.

If you reflect over 'thought communication' and other similar yogic achievements, be sure your spiritual progress will be retarded. If you fail to feel the unseen presence of your Ishta, if you fail to meditate upon him and if you fail to perfect your faith in his divinity, you will only remain a log. What about most of the devotees! Merely saying the beads and thinking of a lot of worldly things!

There is no meaning in having faith in the master only after he has performed certain miracles. What is this funny condition? Real faith and love are independent experiences which you develop even before you know a person. Then what use is it to talk of seeing? Will you have less or no faith in God until you have seen him? Do you say that you will

13

have more faith in God if he comes to you face to face? No, baccha, no! You cannot see him until and unless your faith is complete.

Faith is the first and foremost condition. God-realization is an outcome of intense, unflinching and non-dual faith. Faith does not demand any proof or epistemological conclusions. Faith is that intuitive attitude which one cultivates inwardly even before one comes across an object or a person. Of course, faith presupposes love. Thus we love the object of our faith; then awareness; then merging; finally realization. This is how the whole matter progresses.

Listen, you cannot expect me to demonstrate my divinity to your physical senses. You cannot round me up this way. You are free to renounce me if you fail to induce me to exhibit a tamasha of my divinity in the form of miracles. Be sure that I am not in the least interested in impressing you this way. It is not I who will have to impress you. It is you who will have to realize this divinity of your own accord. Do not detain faith until you are impressed. Better shift the channels and projections of faith and love. If you are not fully convinced about your guru and Govinda, there is absolutely no use in your sadhana.

I am desireless. There is nothing which I aspire to accomplish here and hereafter. There is nothing which I miss in life. I need not do anything. It is for the spiritual aspirants that I come, move and talk. What do I care whether you accept me as your master or not? Is it of any use to perform miracles just to convince the dullheads of your type, especially when eternal, infinite miracles of the Almighty in the cosmos have not opened your eyes? No one has realized the great one through the physical eyes. No one can see him so long as that person is seeing all the rest. No one can hear the divine music so long as he is concerned with worldly tumults. It is only after the external perceptions have been withdrawn and the last of the traces of lower love and passion have also diminished that he comes, sings, loves and makes one blessed.

14

Listen, I do not like to appear in that mind where I do not find non-dual love and complete surrender. Love for the world and worldly objects should not come in my way.

I enter into the chamber alone, allowing no second occupant. I return if I find even a mild trace of dissipation. Yes, I return if I find even a bit of self-consciousness in the lady of the chamber. Indeed, I return if I find the body for me and the mind for the world. Surely, I return if I feel that the nine passages of the chamber are allowing foreign vibrations to have access into it. I return if I don't see the lady looking intently and constantly unto the doors of the chamber. I return even if I see the lady welcoming me while hiding someone else in the innermost chamber.

I look at him who looks at me. I come unto him who comes unto me. I wake up in him who is awake in my awareness. Not the speech but the mind. Nay, not the mind but the soul. Yes, soul – who has offered his soul at the altar of my awareness? Unto him I am given.

If he looks at me with his eyes, he just sees as much as his eyes can. If he thinks of me with his mind, he just thinks as much as the mind can. For the eyes see bodies; the mind perceives thoughts. Who will realize him then? Let the eyes merge in the mind, mind into awareness, ultimately awareness into realization. Let the senses merge in the mind, mind into Ishtam, and Ishtam into darshan.

You want to fly without wings. You want to become a yogini without yoga sadhana. You want to pass the examination without study. Look here, every bit of your personality should be transformed in his awareness so that you express his existence through the mind and senses. He is in you, even as butter is in milk. During every second of twenty years that you have lived, he has constantly been with you. Churn, and the butter will become a reality.

Listen, you will be given what you aspire for. Just rest assured. Do not land your soul into mad thinking. Just do sadhana and materialize the awareness. Nothing more.

15

Empty yourself. Tune your radio. Unite your mind. The rest will take place when the proper time is due.

Thy Lord is in thee. Introvert your eyes, your ears, your mind and the totality of your feelings. And lo, here are cooler sensations; here are hot sensations; here are sudden flashes at times; sudden light at times. Here he comes like a sudden flash of lightning and goes away. Again he comes and overtakes the body consciousness.

At times, tears flow like the Ganga's streams and the physical consciousness is swept away. Suddenly he calls. Attention! Do not open the eyes. At times he sings and you join in his music.

When love becomes overpowering, faith reaches the final point of culmination, then he is in front of you in flesh and blood. Now you can talk to him. You can sit by him. He will reveal unto thee the power of consciousness. He will give you all you ask for. Let the wise one understand this.

No other duty for you. You need not think as to what would happen and how. Sadhana, sadhana and sadhana! Awareness, awareness and awareness! The rest he will do as he deems fit. He may give you the power of healing, or the power of omniscience, or the power to travel through space. However, this is not your concern at all! Don't trouble yourself regarding the fruits. Practice alone is your concern.

In fact, I am eager for that very day when: (a) your consciousness will become intense and keen, (b) you will enter into deep meditation, and (c) you will be able to commune and converse with your Ishtam. That will be the day of a great festivity, a day of real joy. And the great spiritual power to help, lift and elevate others will be conferred upon thee. Your prayers will be answered.

I have already accepted you as my divine child. May you sing the song of truth unto all like Chaitanya and Mira!

There is no harm in shedding tears in his love, but that must not break the theme of consciousness. Nothing that disturbs the consciousness should be done. Anything which develops a focused state of mind should be accepted readily.

Please remember that you need not try to observe how you are feeling during sadhana. There should be nothing left in the mind except name and form. Physical sensations, coolness, lightness, etc. are such feelings that they take the mental consciousness away from the goal. Even if you see a light, hear a sound, or experience rainy showers, or feel jerks, or feel like becoming unconscious, you should be careful that you don't drift away from name and form. These signs are just the indications of growing one-pointedness of the mind. They reveal to the sadhaka that he should be still more aware of name and form. Those yogic experiences which you have enumerated are the signs of growing mental poise in you. You need not attempt to recollect those experiences.

Raipur, February 15, 1958

Thy promising letter. I am glad that you have at last gained faith in your guru. In fact, you have gained faith in God and thyself. Guru, God and thyself are *essentially* one. If only you have perfected faith, you can work miracles. Intensity of faith (unmindful of any amount of failures) is the only condition which will convert thy soul into the divine. Let not any amount of failures depress thy heart; and let not success snatch from thee thy mental equilibrium.

Life is a series of successes and failures. There are none who can claim to be an exception to this law. You are a new visitor here in this mortal soil. What you should do is to be adamant and enduring in the hailstorms, tempests and temptations of life. Offer every joy to thy master, to thy God. In fact, our sorrow and joy are nothing; our individual exaggerated fantasy makes them appear magnified a thousandfold.

So long as you have not attained the highest, you will continue to feel various pleasant and unpleasant sensations. So long as you are a victim of ambitions and discontent, you

17

will continue to experience positive and negative charges of those sensations. And, so long as you maintain the least trace of uncertainty in your soul, you will experience headaches, restlessness and a peculiar panic in your heart.

It is only when you have kicked off and thrown aside all good and evil wants and desires, doubts and brooding, every fear of being spoilt and scared and insulted and praised, that you will become the happiest person in the world. Let thy body live in the world; let thy atma rest in God. Merge your thoughts and desires in God. This is the key to paramananda or supreme joy.

It is only after you have realized that you are an immortal child playing an eternal lila in the lap of eternity that you will really become happy. Feel the blessings of your Divine Father. Know that you are being protected at every step of your life by a strange mendicant. Intensify your spiritual receptivity so as to catch the waves of his affection and particular care showered upon you.

Girls have to be mentally strong, not merely careful. They have to overhaul the very system of their behaviour, expression and conversation. Dignity of soul they must possess. While understanding the weakness of other members, let girls give no room to its expression.

What I see is that the innocent and tender mental constitution of girls unconsciously gives room and license to be easily hypnotized by other members. Girls are invariably overcome by slight efforts; and when the process of overwhelming is complete, they have to submit and yield. Since girls have by their very nature more suppressed emotions, they are easily assailed by obligations and favours done to them. Generally, the process begins with hearty appreciation of the other party, which is followed by contemplation. At this critical moment, she can be made to yield easily.

Well, if matters ended with this much, one would not bother further. What happens afterwards you know. A regular series of accidents, mental and social insanity, hysteria and

18

delusions, frustrations, so on and so forth. Nervous and psychological disorders ensue. Disgust prevails over life. Animal passions rise high. Self-confidence is totally lost. Consequently she develops an abnormal personality, and thus (poor chap!) life drags on with bitter memories of an ungratified past and fears of an uncertain, unlucky future.

The jiva remains a victim of maya until one becomes divine. This maya has natural magnetism. It is the central point of gravity in our emotional body. So, I am lovingly suggesting that you create around yourself an anti-magnetic condition by a reserved, peaceful and holy behaviour and character, by a simple, unostentatious yet clever disposition. You must have moral courage. Throw off mental fears. Keep the holy gift of God, this human life, unsullied, unscathed and ever divine. Wake up Rama, you are essentially pure, enlightened and taintless. You are far from the maya of this world (the burden of mental conflicts).

Love all. Did I ask you to love physically? I only asked you to stop reflecting over others' misbehaviour, jealousy and evil nature. Harbour no thought against anyone in thy mind. I didn't mean that you should submit and yield, shampoo and flatter, beg pardon and sell away thy soul. No and never. Love is a spiritual experience of the inner being. It's another name for strong and tolerant dedication. It can be best expressed in the service of mankind. Servants of mankind know best the art of loving. It is also one's inner attitude for God and guru. Love can be better practised by keeping the soul under philosophical control.

Perfection, which you seek after, is a spiritual pinnacle of the soul; it is not just material. If your mind remains unruffled; if lower appetites don't trouble you; if you meditate regularly; if the past doesn't interfere with your present stage of head, heart and hands; if you are regular in japa and kirtan; if you have implicit faith in your guru and God; and if you consider God as your eternal and inseparable companion, then alone can you reach the summit of perfection. Perfect social behaviour, of course, provides us

19

with the conditions wherein we can fully experience the joy of spiritual perfection.

You are successfully marching towards perfection. I visualize it vividly. May you keep the zeal of sadhana ever fresh!

Never should you miss japa, kirtan and meditation. Never should you fail to feel the presence of God within you. God is not *only* nirakara. He is not *only* an abstract reality. He is like you and like me as well. He is as well sitting by your side. He is a healing doctor and a loving partner of life. You must strive to see him this way; and seek His grace. Guru and God are *one*. Both of them move like ordinary mortals and help their devotees. Remove your mental screen of avidya and dispel the inertia; you can move his heart.

And, I reveal to thee that none except a bhakta is really happy. I have been coming across numerous individuals belonging to various walks of life, but have not come across even a single happy soul as yet. Avidya causes darkness. Darkness causes fear. Fear causes confusion. Confusion causes objects. Objects cause craving. Craving causes indulgence. Indulgence causes samskaras. Samskaras cause birth and death and again rebirth. These three cause unhappiness and unrest in the depth of the soul. So, in order to be really happy, one has to cut the very roots of avidya by dint of bhakti sadhana as taught by one's gurudev.

Worldly objects won't give you lasting happiness. You shouldn't be enamoured of their quixotic fancies and magnifications. As a witness transcend the realms of maya. Live in the world as a lotus leaf lives in water; as the tongue lives in between two sets of sharp teeth; as Shiva lives in the wilderness of life. Live you must; but realize this truth about life at all costs. Until you have evolved and learnt, you must face this world. Master the school first; and then renounce. Renunciation will come to thy door when the time is ripe and when you are prepared.

A simple life is a veritable blessing because it makes one free from cravings and desires, which cause suffering and pain. So long as one is bound to this pain born of cravings and desires, it is quite difficult to experience God. Pain which is born of lower hunger is terrible. It kills the very essence of man. So has it been said that simplicity opens the gates which lead to heaven and God.

Simple you ought to be, but never foolish; for simplicity is not that condition of life where one is easily duped and deceived by others. Saints are simplicity personified. Does it mean that they are ignorant of events occurring around them? No. They are fully aware of what is happening around them. So please don't equate simple life with 'ignorant and foolish' life.

You can lead a simple life by simplifying your mental mechanism which is responsible for inner conflicts. You can be simple by reducing your desires for unnecessary dresses, food and ornaments. You can lead a life of simplicity while performing your official as well as domestic duties. The best way to be simple is to give up: (a) repenting, (b) worrying, (c) brooding, (d) weeping for unfulfilled desires and (e) indulging in anti-psychological and anti-religious thoughts and behaviours.

Simplicity of external conditions is easiest. Simplicity of speech is marvellous. Simplicity of thought is an unparalleled virtue. Wear coarse khadi or simple, plain and white dresses. Gradually give up the use of silk and the like. Silk produces physical extroversion, consequently love for passion. One should dress decently, but not daintily and uselessly. Give up the use of cosmetics of all kinds if at all you are doing so. Simple hair oil is the only scent allowed for sadhakas. Go deeper and realize why I advise you on these lines.

Repetition of the name is divine 'bangles and rings'. Sadhana is the best of all beautifying agents. Japa is a never-fading lipstick. Yoga is the only pancake which can produce everlasting lustre. Annihilation of 'ego' is the real process of taking a wash. Can soap clean the dirt of our soul?

Investigate real faith in God while performing all the duties to the best of your capacities. Faith knows no defeat,

21

no frustration and no 'stop' order. Suspense and uncertainty do not trouble one who has faith. Let no effort be spared; let no failure be inwardly felt.

Be in tune with holy thoughts in the morning and at night. Calm the mind; pacify your thoughts. Visualize your Ishta by you or in front of you. Try to feel a pleasant sensation passing through every part of your being. Let love be the essential basis of your dhyana. God is at once your father, brother and all. Select any of these bhavas according to your liking and then tune your mind for divine vibrations.

My blessings are always with you and within you. You can feel me and my good wishes in the very soul of your being. You can commune with me during meditation. You can materialize the guru and God in flesh and blood wherever you want and whenever you want.

Bhagalpur, May 12, 1958

Destroy passion, anger and irritability. Will you remain a true brahmacharini and karma yogini? You *can,* if you have determined strongly. Temptations will be too many; but I am sure you will try your best to overcome them. Your love for God and faith in his mercy as well as my good wishes will help you to walk upon this path of supermen.

Young age is the proper time to reap the divine harvest. While you are healthy, young, energetic and fresh, offer yourself unto him. What is the use of offering an old, rotten flower, with no beauty and fragrance? Give him your mind; give to the world the body. Give him your soul; give the world your hands and senses.

Life is an experiment. Nature is performing it. She moulds, fashions, refashions, breaks and joins the jiva through various methods in various lives. Life is a school where we study.

Don't go to any ashram, math or mandir. You have asked me 'to lead thee on'. He has assigned me this task. Have

22

faith in one God, one guru, one mantra, one religion and
one method of sadhana. Dissipate not hither and thither.

Amarkantak, May 25, 1958

You are walking all right. You will realize your real swarupa.
Still you have to walk a lot. Every step should be taken
cautiously.

Practise the sadhanas necessary for pratyahara. Side by
side concentrate on your Ishta devata. The Lord will manifest
his spiritual being during your meditation and bless you
with darshan, divine experience and jnana. Japa will lead
your psyche to the plane of astral consciousness; and
concentration itself will culminate into meditation.

Meditation will open the doors of *power* for thee. Hence
you must do japa, concentration and meditation with absolute
one-pointedness. Tune thy mind. Create receptivity. If only
you have tuned your radio, you will be given the knowledge
during your meditation.

Concentrate on the form until your mental tendencies
have become focused and all other thoughts have ceased. It
is only then that guru and disciple can commune with each
other in the plane of spiritual consciousness.

So long as there are various conflicts and imaginary
complexes in your personality, you will be missing your guru
in meditation. No sooner have your mental activities merged
into a single spiritual awareness or sumiran than you can
materialize your guru consciousness and commune.

You don't see me because of defective sense-vision. No
sooner have you transcended the body consciousness than
you can certainly contact me within the psychic plane. You
will develop this art of inner communion within a short
period, provided you are sincere and regular in your yoga
sadhana.

You have been already initiated. You have a guru. There
is no doubt about your success.

23

You should not even imagine renouncing home because of certain responsibilities which you yourself have imagined. Religion which is born of failures and shirking of responsibilities will not carry you further any more. You have felt certain responsibilities heavily. You have certain emotions unfulfilled. So you feel like getting out of the net. Will you listen to me and change your present attitude towards this world? Instead of brooding over this world, better saturate your being in his love. If you have faith in guru, you must face this world so long as he wants. Remain in the society, earn money, run hither and thither and meditate twice a day.

I am your guru, your marga bandhu. Remember thy spiritual mantra. Do not lose sight of thy road. You need not renounce; you need not roam. My blessings are always with you. Try to experience and follow them.

Rajnandgaon, July 1, 1958

Today is Guru Poornima. Let our hearts be enlightened with the light of true knowledge. Satyam wishes you holy blessings on this day. May you celebrate this day with purity, love and devotion!

On this occasion I once again draw your conscious attention to the aim of life. Besides all that you are doing, be ever aware of what you are living for. You will have to experience; you will have to realize your Lord in this life itself.

I don't ask you to renounce duties and home. It is not quite necessary for you or for anyone to renounce home for the sake of God-realization. You will have to awaken in your heart an unshakeable faith and supreme love for your Lord.

Your soul is all-powerful. Your Lord is also all-powerful. He is within you. You will be able to meet him in meditation. He will come to you in flesh and blood. He will talk to you. He will take you by his hand. When one rises above body

24

consciousness in meditation, then the inner Lord manifests. He will come to you. You will feel his loving and divine presence. Strengthen your faith on the occasion of Guru Poornima.

You have been already given a law, a dharma, a sadhana, a faith by his grace, which you should constantly uphold. You are expected to be earnest and true to your sadhana, God and guru. And nobody in the world should be able to shatter your noble faith and philosophical convictions.

From now on it is not at all necessary for you to attend satsangs, or services in a temple, or a congregation in an ashram. That part of your sadhana is over. You have gone a step further. If you still continue to attend different satsangs at this stage of sadhana, there is every chance for great confusion to overpower your mind. Different intellectual principles will puzzle you; and you may even doubt your spiritual practices. Instead, devote that much time in sadhana. Enough of reading scriptures. If you perfect your sadhana, deepen the faith and attain the heights of meditation, you will see the scriptures revealed even without any outer or intellectual efforts.

Be studious. Be pure. Be happy. Read less. Meditate more. Enough of scriptural studies. No amount of reading will give you realization. Meditation alone will take you to him. Restart spiritual practices with a new vigour. Blessings of the Brahma Vidya Gurus!

Rajnandgaon, August 27, 1958

Thy monthly report. Let the mind get fused in your Ishta Devata. When the fusion is perfect, then your sankalpa will become dynamic. You will heal the sick. You will get higher knowledge. When your Lord remains no more a symbol, but instead expresses himself before you as it were in flesh and blood, it is then that wisdom dawns and jnana is attained. It is a fact. It is certainly possible for you to materialize the physical body of a person whom you have never met before. Of course, only in deepest dhyana.

I have made it a point to charge you daily with energy and willpower. The moment your sadhana is complete, I shall transfer the power. Be in tune with me in meditation.

No sooner is the mind consumed by one form than external sounds cease; and none but one is experienced. It is then that the knowledge, power and light are transferred.

You don't require a special place. You can practise this even in an easy chair. Thus others would not even know that you are immersed in meditation. If your faith is intense and single-pointed, you will speedily enter into meditation.

Brahmacharya in thought, speech and practice helps a great deal. Brooding is a great obstacle. Don't get disturbed by noise, etc. This is a test of your progress. It is only after the external sounds have stopped irritating you that you should realize you have really made initial progress. Never until then.

When this stage is arrived at, your *will* will begin to work as if it were a physical power. The Gita and other scriptures will be revealed unto thee. I am prepared to help you even from this distance.

It is not essential that we should meet personally. Personal contact doesn't mean that our spirits have necessarily united. Union of spirits is possible even in the absence of that person. Reflect over this fundamental truth.

Rajnandgaon, October 7, 1958

Do you remember your prayer? "Let us bet, O Lord, as to who has more patience. I can wait at thy door for years and ages, but you can't have the patience to keep thy bhakta out waiting at thy door for long!"

I am very pleased to learn from your letter that you are full with joy and ananda. God is param ananda swarupa. Yes, you should speedily transform chinta into sumiran and dukha into ananda. Your aspirations are right and sublime.

Your faith is deep, intense and unshakeable. Your devotion is unique. Only one virtue remains to be acquired – *transform emotions into divine love.*

Love! It is an inexplicable attitude towards one's Ishta devata. It is not passion, not lust, not romance. It is an unceasing thirst, unforgettable remembrance and eternal application for uniting with one's Ishta. Love is not madness. Love is constant awareness. Do you understand?

So long as one has attraction towards worldliness, one just remains an ordinary devotee. Love intensifies remembrance. Constant remembrance transforms the love into darshan. Love is not a duty. Love is the totality of dedication.

It is good that you have placed God in your inner chamber, reserving the whole chamber for him and locked up its gates from inside with a big Godrej lock of dhyana. It is now that the knowledge shall be revealed unto thee. Are you sure about his presence there?

You will be able to talk to me in dhyana as soon as your consciousness becomes calm and peaceful. Tune your radio. Lo, the music is there.

Yes, it is possible to know anything in meditation, but why should you waste your energy and time? Know God in meditation. Meditate daily, regularly, punctually.

I have received your 'rakhi' as a symbol of prayer for protection. I shall always protect thee from whirlpools, tempests and dark forces. Smile, laugh and dance in divine joy; your father is ever by your side.

I am glad to know that you have not minimized your efficiency and that you do your office job well. That should be the spirit of love and dedication.

Bhakti does not lie in renunciation. It is a limitless expression of one's all-round talents. Religion doesn't ask one to give up day to day duties. It only asks you to get rid of mental imbalance, moral evils and spiritual ignorance. Bhakti exhorts ceaseless engagements from morning till night. Fie be upon that wretch who underrates the value of work in the name of tyaga.

What I want is to awaken the soul. What I want of you is to realize thy prestige and glory. Thou art not a girl, a target of animal passion and a victim of romantic shows. Thou art not this physical body meant for exploitation. Thou art that spirit which, when awakened, can move immovable mountains, bring the dead back to life, bestow sight to the blind and command nature. Beloved child of truth thou art! Even as Sri Rama incarnated in a human form, even as Lord Krishna appeared and played with cowherd boys, likewise you are amidst clerks, officers, relatives and ignorant men and women. Never forget this great truth, *That thou art*.

Now, regarding sadhana. You are doing well. Do concentrate on the form. If you merely meditate on ideas, either particular or associated, you might land somewhere else also. Concentration on a form is easy and important.

If you can't recollect the form in your mind, then bank upon the photo alone for some time. Meditation on associated thoughts alone will not give you concentration. This is just to prepare the background for a peaceful sitting. Always make it a point to start concentration with a good background. Select one of the poses for the purpose of concentration. Don't change it, even if it does not get clearer for some time.

What was that form of your Ishtam which became clearer on the 17th? Choose that one; why not? What exactly I want to bring to your mind is the necessity of sticking to *one form*. Concentration on various poses will disturb the mental patterns before each one of them becomes permanent.

Success is not too far now. You will have to merge the mind in *one form*. Meditation is neither manbahalava nor thinking various thoughts. Meditation is that state when your mind becomes ek-rupa with *one form*. See your Ishtam in that same pose everywhere. Do not depend much upon associated thoughts. It is only when the mind wanders too much that you can think of the associated divine thoughts. You can reflect over associated thoughts in your spare time also; but during sadhana, meditate on *one form* alone. You will get success as soon as you take refuge in *one form*. Do not disturb the consciousness by changing over form and posture for concentration. Pray, you understand this. Tell me, on which form do you meditate?

Do sit in vajrasana, sukhasana and padmasana one after another. But aim at padmasana ultimately. Practise other yoga asanas with closed eyes and slowly. Don't practise yogic asanas, except padma and vajra, during monthly periods. Do you experience weakness by doing asanas?

Don't waste Sundays in socials or chakkar baji. How many Sundays have been wasted so far! Utilize this day in mouna, japa and dhyana. Never give up japa. Let it continue along with concentration also. Perform asanas twice on Sundays. Keep the mind calm, quiet and serene on Sundays. There is no end to friendly invitations. Ye sadhaka, thy destination is far, far, still far; sail thy boat quickly. Don't waste even a single moment.

Delhi, November 27, 1958

Why don't you do japa at night also? Japa is a positive method of 'mental silence'. Give up the habit of merely sitting or lying quiet. One can't do it because the inner mind is always active, except when one meditates or does japa. Sit outside in the open by all means. But don't dream please. That will undo your achievements. Close your eyes; sing his names; and then do japa. You can do it inside the room also. There will be less disturbance. Anyway, learn the real art of *sitting quiet*.

Let me congratulate you on your poem of devotion, which I have just received. The real and most obstinate poem is the *form*, which you will have to compose and manifest. Meditation is the sweetest poem. When the psychic night dawns and *that* silence prevails, unfold thy inner poetry, thy soul, yes, that form! Can you?

When will the form become clearer? Shall I tell you? It is only after your mind has finally selected a single form. At present your mind is wandering amidst various forms and postures. It has not yet merged in a single form. There is still a lot of disturbance in the mansarovar.

One sadhana more. 'Fearlessness'. How to become fearless? Never indulge in such talks, never do such acts and never keep such things which you have to hide from others. In the beginning you may find it a bit difficult; but by and by everything will become possible. Secret talks, secret letters, secret relations, secret affairs, all these give birth and strength to a fear complex.

Fear breaks the organized pattern of mind which was formed in meditation. Fear weakens the willpower. So long as you carry on with such works which you want to hide from others, you have to be afraid. So long as fear exists in you, your willpower will not function and bear fine fruits. Therefore, you should speak such things, do such acts, talk with such persons and have such correspondence which you would not feel like hiding from others. This is a sure aid to success in spiritual life.

You will have to mould your life also side by side with meditation. Are there conflicts still in your mind? Either say you haven't any, or else express where the shoe bites. What lurks in thee as a conflict? What is that which you are lacking in life and which upsets you off and on? I stand by your side under all odd moments.

I know your troubles. But by telling them yourself, you will only relax your mental constipation and hypertension. At the back the thief hides. In the forefront you don't see it. Tell thy troubles to him, although he already knows all; for by saying them yourself you will become lighter and free. Understand this psychological truth. Don't deceive your own self by addressing your guru, *"You already know"*. It is an erroneous and self-deceptive expression. Whether I know or not, how are you concerned? You have to purge out what lurks in *your* mind. God knows all; yet we speak out our minds unto him just to express ourselves and lay down the mental burden before him.

I assure you that I will protect you and accept your mental burden. You just speak out your mind to me liberally, even if you have to write a hundred pages per day. I will never consider that as silly and rubbish. Well, even if that be silly and rubbish, better it comes out sooner. Be that rubbish or sensible, silly or good, it must be thrown out of the mind. Vacate all psychic compartments of this filth of fermented and suppressed vasanas. Then also shall that be refilled with divine grace.

I want you to speak out your mind, purge all the rubbish and get rid of the mental constipation. Hurry up and evacuate the mind in toto. I will never misunderstand your bhava, your purging and your emotions. I am your mother. I won't mind at all even if you abuse me. I know that would do you immense good.

Amravati, December 15, 1958

Let people laugh, scorn, or do as they like. Why do you forget your aim? Anxious to know what others might be thinking? This causes adversity. Adversity is rampant everywhere. You cannot eliminate it. Adversity is one's own creation. The best way is to face it. I do not understand what exactly is creating a sort of disgust in you for your present work. Why do you want to be away from it? I can only say one thing. Be strong; still more strong!

Remember that your present job and life are nothing but stepping stones towards a great mission and that trifling things are creating a nuisance in your mind. If this sort of thing lurks in your mind, what can I expect of you? Has it not been said that pains and adversities are testing stones for our willpower and faith?

Let not these trifling events disturb you. They are mere vibrations, mere opinions and mere jealousy. Nothing solid and nothing sound. None can kill you, you know. Why are you receptive to unwanted events then?

31

Nothing would disturb you if you focus your attention on God. You will succeed and come out with victory in any work you take up. You can remove the impediments from your way by a single utterance of prayer. The crisis which you are facing presently will pass away very soon. But do promise me that you will hereafter never allow the creation of a similar crisis to arise and that you will keep your life clean.

And again, this sort of mental disturbance born of frustration, desperation, etc. is a great barrier in your spiritual progress. You will have to constantly remember that mental equilibrium in day to day life enhances sadhana and accelerates spiritual progress. Day to day dislocation of the peaceful mental structure creates conflicts in the mind which, in turn, hinder the meditational process. Therefore, we do not err in the first place and if at all we do, we do not repeat it again. We never repent. If there is any tumult on the astral plane, we place it at the feet of our master.

If you cannot realize God wherever you might be, be sure you will not be able to realize him anywhere else in spite of all the illumined souls leading you on your path.

What a funny thing! A little scandal can break the peace of your soul? A little something can create disgust for the world, while I would have expected you to laugh at the scandals and remove your tension by faithful prayer unto the Lord. Still there is a chance. You can reorganize yourself.

Delhi, December 30, 1958

Now that you have decided the form of your Ishtam for concentration, please commence an eleven day anushthana starting from 3rd January and completing on the night of the 13th. During this period you will have to maintain perpetual sadhana consciousness; no break may be allowed.

Adjust this way. Get up at 3.45 a.m. Repeat the name at once and start recollecting that form of your Ishtam which

32

you have finally chosen. Side by side take your bath. Practise asanas up to 5 a.m. Now have a sitting for 'japa sahita dhyana' as long as possible.

Then prepare yourself for the office while repeating the mantra mentally. Do japa while you are in the train.

As soon as you return from the office, recline and relax. Have a sitting at night, so long as it is possible.

In short, during these eleven days intensify the sadhana (japa and dhyana) to its climax and have a few mystic experiences.

Special instructions
- Be calm, cool, serene and dispassionate.
- Talk less and work efficiently.
- Be above criticism.
- No trace of passion to be felt.
- Feel inner happiness, strength and bliss.
- Don't attend social functions and parties.
- Be above worries and weariness.

Think nothing except the repetition and remembrance of name and form.

You will experience sudden flashes of light preceded by hot sensations on the face and fingers. It will happen almost daily in your morning meditation. You will dream the form on some night.

You will dream as if a sweet note of 'Om Nama Shivaya' is being sung. Following the song you will get up.

By the 10th day, concentration will become keen; you will dream his form with glow, light and flowers.

Don't be afraid of hot sensations, lights, sounds, smells, etc. They will come and go away. Even if you see ugly and fearful figures, you shouldn't mind. You should always keep the awareness of your Ishtam before you.

So you have understood most of the theories. You have to be relentless at the practice. With these practices, together with faith, love and sincerity, you will reach the goal.

As desired, we shall meet on the 6th at 5.30 a.m. Be in tune with me. Switch on the inner current. Don't be afraid. Listen to yourself first; then only myself. Please be seated on a deerskin only.

Geographical distance is no barrier. We shall meet when the senses and mind have gone to sleep and when we two stand on an equal footing. That is the plane of atma. Will you climb up these staircases? Climb them one by one, until you are able to enter into daharakasha. It is there that we will meet on the 6th at 5.30 a.m.

Please be in tune with me on the 15th, 16th and 17th. Start your sadhana at 5 a.m. itself, so that by 5.30 a.m. the ground for receptivity might be somewhat clearer. Don't get afraid and disheartened at any cost. You will have to be intensely aware of your Ishtam and mantra. That is all. You need not strive to know as to what I might be transmitting. *Please follow it properly.*

If your mind is in tune with nama and rupa, you will be able to receive anything I will be transmitting. But if you try to put yourself in direct communication with those transmissions at this stage, you will not succeed. When the mind merges in his consciousness, then the receptivity becomes spontaneous and automatic. After all, what I might transmit is already in your inner mind. What you have to do is exactly this: tune the mind and merge that same tuned mind in your Ishtam.

I will not be sending many calls. Just one theme; a simple theme every day. On the 17th, of course, I will be transmitting a series of linked thoughts, like a chain.

Please don't use silken dresses during your sittings. Fast on the previous night. Take every precaution to safeguard your mind from disturbing factors of every nature. Please dry your hair perfectly before you sit for the reception. Do not at all forget the use of the deerskin. No earth contact during the period. Remove rings, tops and hairpins as well as other metals from the body.

You have written about your thought materialization. Right, but don't be egoistic. As your sadhana gets intense, you will have many such miraculous experiences. Your thoughts will materialize to your surprise. You will be able to read others' minds also. But don't raise your head. Always be humble. Siddhis will meet you on the way, but beware, you have to go further.

A tired and weary traveller came under the shade of a kalpa taru to rest. He wished for some water, for he was very thirsty. Wonder! He got the water to drink. Then he thought of sleeping. Lo, he got a fine bed also to sleep in. In the evening, when he looked around the wild forest, he became frightened of the forest animals. Lo, a tiger came and devoured him.

The mind of a sadhaka is the kalpa taru. The feelings rising in the mind ocean become converted into spiritual power. If the sadhaka's mind is full of faith, fearlessness, hope and goodness, he receives infinite boons. If he gets frightened in adverse conditions and loses the precious faith, he is lost and he is doomed.

Your mind is growing into a kalpa taru. You must have only two wills at present. Firstly, darshan of chinmaya vigraha; secondly, strength for mental balance at every stage of life. Other thoughts will have to be thought, decided and disposed of by your external mind only. The vital mind, the seat of consciousness, must only have the above-mentioned two thoughts. Exercise your willpower for spiritual progress only.

Yet caution! About what? Caution about your destination. You are going on a pilgrimage. You will come across rivers, hills, deserts and wilderness. You will come across a caravansarai, conducted by craving and attachment, assisted by desire, etc. You will also come across a beautiful garden laden with beautiful flowers and shady trees, owned by materialism and science. And since you have already decided to follow your guide on this pilgrimage, keep on following him.

Allahabad, January 11, 1959

Prayer is a direct connection between God and devotee. Every prayer is heard and fulfilled. Pray with all love, humility and confidence! God is always receptive to prayers.

Chapra (Bihar), February 2, 1959

Right understanding of inner light dawns only in dhyana. Transcend the body and mind. Now you can experience the true bliss. You are purity. You are an embodiment of sadhana. You are an expression of the divine.

Thine atma is thy eternal companion. He is in thee, beside thee and everywhere. Get closer to him in meditation. For one has not the eyes to see him in the world of senses; one has not the senses to experience his nearness in sense consciousness.

The world goes on as it should. We act only as instruments. It is always wise and safe to renounce egoistic spirit. Let it happen, if it happens and as it happens. Never worry over anything. Events take their destined course automatically. You are not to break your head. You are just to cooperate in the plan.

Be up and doing. Be regular in your yoga. Be faithful. Realize God as quickly as possible. Faith in sadhana, guru and truth is essential for self-realization; hence, perfect your faith.

I am glad to go through your experiences in meditation. I am sending spiritual currents daily in the morning.

36

There is no love greater than faith. There is no reverence greater than obedience. There is no bliss greater than the bliss of meditation. There is none greater than one's divine shepherd.

Let the day come when you would become the master of your mind. Even as you see, hear and walk in dreams, although your senses are locked, likewise will you see, hear and know anything you desire. The mind is capable of spanning the gulfs between past, present and future. What it needs is proper training and guidance in spiritual practices.

Always remember
- that you will not exert in sadhana; meditation is spontaneous culmination of dharana; divine love easily leads one to meditation;
- that you will not rest until the form manifests life and reality;
- that you will not succumb to those obstacles enumerated in the last 'Initiation Paper';
- that no amount of visions should take you off the track of Ishta sadhana; and
- that you will take proper mental and physical rest.

These visions which you have described in your letter are signs of mental unification to a great extent. They do come, up to a particular stage of sadhana. However, they shouldn't allure the sadhaka and distract him from his path of Ishta rupa sadhana.

Lights and visions are inner symptoms of the consummation of mental vrittis. They indicate that your various mental waves are merging in the ocean of your chosen form or Ishta Devata.

Still, that is not your goal. Your goal is to cast the entire store of mental stuff into the pattern of your Ishtam. That is to say, your mind must cease to be your mind. It should become one with shuddha manas. Then alone will dawn a commonness in two minds. Two minds will become alike. This is what you will experience by merging yourself in this form.

At this moment no other thought except the thought of routine work should occupy your mind. So far as the thoughts regarding sadhana are concerned, they should be just that, "My Lord's form is like this; his voice is like this; and his form must become conscious."

You needn't analyze the philosophy of lights. Even as a traveller leaves the last milestone to reach the fresh one, likewise past experiences should not be recollected. There is only one thing which is the main object of your concern: that is the manifestation of the form during deep meditation, when the witness of meditation and meditator have embraced each other. There will come a stage when you will not witness the experiences during meditation even.

You must have a risk free place for meditation. Study the last 'Initiation Paper' and make a note of the phenomena just before darshan. Yes, you must have a deerskin. That will absorb the psychic electricity and maintain the continuity of form.

There will come a stage when you will recollect your experiences only after you have come out of meditation. At the present stage of meditation, a part of your mind becomes a seer while the rest becomes the seen. That is why you witness the entire process of meditation during sadhana. Try to forget yourself completely by maintaining a secular attitude towards visions and lights and psychic sensations. By and by the visions will slow down, and the consciousness of form alone will reign supreme. Ultimately, the subject and object too will merge in one.

No doubt, a stomach condition does come in one's way for dhyana; but you needn't worry about it at all, since you are practising yogic asanas as well.

Have intense faith that 'everything will become all right'. Don't worry and break your head. Just plan and do things in an efficient and regular manner. Thinking and reasoning differ from worrying and troubling the mind. Think and decide; don't worry and tax the mind. Efficiency, intelligence and interest need be neither eliminated nor even minimized.

38

Continue to be a speedometer in your normal and routine work. God is great. He will always help you.

Don't get up at 2 a.m. Proper rest is essential for sadhakas. You must train your mind to give you a caution just at 4 a.m. Your mind is sure to obey you without any flaw.

If you can't realize and achieve the divine knowledge while you are at home, I assure you that you can't do it anywhere else. The freedom, the homeliness and the security which one enjoys at home are absolutely absent in any ashram. Not only ladies, even males experience insecurity and a unhomely atmosphere there. Lots of artificiality comes in one's behaviour. None can realize God in an ashram if he fails to do it at home.

If one has a guide to show the path, what more does one need? Ekanta and ceaseless meditation. One can virtually lead a life of seclusion by withdrawing the mind from diversity and by fixing it to *one*. One must practise ceaseless meditation also. Know that no ashram has ever produced a superman. Supermen are the products of ceaseless sadhana, purification, concentration and unification.

Yes, you are a magazine of power. Behind the flesh, pranas, mind and subconscious there is something in you which is all-powerful and all-pervading. That something is Purusha. It is known as Ishwara, Rama, Atma, Govinda and is the essence of all that is known variously.

The essence of existence (creation) is *that* which is in thee. The essence of thy existence is that which is enveloped by avidya, kama, karma, impurity and similar other mental cloaks.

This atma, which you are, has the first cloak of avidya, the second cloak of bhrama and the third cloak of samskara.

This atma, which you are, becomes manifest in that state, wherein all cloaks have been torn asunder, aptly known as samadhi.

This atma, which you are, becomes manifest either in one's guru, or Ishta Devata, as soon as the sadhaka has united with the same.

39

Never should primitive ignorance once again dawn upon you. You have already cast off the screen. Lives after lives are going to be revealed to you. Within you is the historical and microscopic film of aeons and ages, mankind and creation. There is nothing which you are not. And so plod on with that undaunted spirit of Arjuna, in the arena of war and peace, struggle and treaty, nivritti and pravritti, work and meditation; until the war is entirely fought and the victory ultimately gained. Every success to you!

Bhagalpur, April 20, 1959

Mental thoughts are created by desires. No sooner than the inner storms subside, the waves are no more. Mind becomes waveless, calm, infinite. It is at this stage that you reach a vision. It is at this stage that you transcend body consciousness. Our effort is to render the mind waveless, calm, serene and infinite by one-pointed perception of the form. This becomes possible when love of God is coupled with yoga.

I am very glad to learn from you that you have already started the anushthana. This anushthana will make your consciousness calm, quiet and serene. Please follow all those regulations essential for anushthana. Please make it a point to repeat the anushthana once every month.

Should you be a little more careful, I assure you that every anushthana will give you a further push. Anushthanas purify the mind, pacify the emotions, amplify bhakti, intensify awareness and help the sadhaka to merge in him.

When everything has been said, anushthanas should be observed with great care, vigilance and guidance. Even a little mistake can do some harm. In the light of this knowledge, I hope you will never relax the restrictions which form a part of anushthana.

Please do not meditate without a deerskin and in silken garments. The rest you know.

Be calm my child and be peaceful. The spiritual path is beset with opposition. Nothing new with you. God alone sends these trials.

Analyze the state of your mind. Has it maintained serenity in spite of test and trials, or has it got broken into pieces of emotions, brooding and rash behaviour? Do not lend your ears to the world when you are right. You have to remain in the world. Apart from all this and that, your behaviour should not go against the interest of family. Have perfect faith in him. Let him do as he wants.

Let me repeat again. *Be calm and be peaceful.*

The spiritual path is very easy for those who know the art of mental equilibrium in all seasons. Merely visiting sadhus and getting initiation, or witnessing miracles will not do. When you board the train, do place your burden on it also. Right alone will happen. His will alone will prevail.

Be calm and be peaceful. Reorganize your inner mechanism of mental serenity which has been shattered and distorted. Dive deep. Meditate and experience his divine presence and blessings.

Never wish ill to anyone. Don't even criticize your opponents. Since you have now been successfully practising yoga, any evil thoughts might well harm your opponents. Pray unto him to bless *everyone* with happiness and peace.

God is in you. He is hidden. Guru is also God, and God is revealed by sadhana and kripa. Guru can do everything; still one has to suffer for one's past karmas. If siddha gurus misuse their omnipotence by interfering in the scheme of karmas, then the great laws will be broken.

Guru has to know the karmas of a man first; and then only help him. Gurus come to awaken the jiva from the deep sleep of ignorance. The jiva gradually wakes up, masters his mind and exhausts the fruits of his past deeds. It is only then that he really becomes happy.

Guru *can* make his disciple free from the laws of karmas, but you know the disciple will indulge once again in the same rotten activities. Therefore, gurus let nature transform life through suffering of all kinds. If the disciple does sadhana and thereby changes his mind, then he has not to suffer anymore. Either he has to suffer the disease and improve his ways of living thereby; or else he has to learn from wise men the ways of good health much before he has begun to suffer.

Gurus come to show the right way. The whole of this truth will be revealed to you after realization. Do not wrack your brain. You can't see a virus without the help of a microscope. In the same way, many things can't be perceived by intellect alone. You will be able to discover the great secrets by guru's upadesha and meditation.

Mount Abu, June 5, 1959

Install a yogic telephone exchange by entering into deep samadhi. Complete the work of wiring gradually; then you can contact vishwatman. The object of meditation must become as clear as reality.

Yes, it can happen. It is only then that you can be a master of occult powers. It is only then that you can have a thorough knowledge of time, space and matter.

Behind the barrier of sense consciousness or indriya anubhuti, there is a field of inner awareness or atma anubhuti. It is there that you have to connect yourself.

Deeper into the soul is the permanent abode of truth. Beyond senses, pranas, sense experiences and feelings is atma chetana.

God consciousness and self-awareness are synonymous.

Constant japa; then concentration; then meditation; then samadhi; nothing further. One form of one kind and one life.

42

Success in samadhi depends upon merging; merging upon constant awareness; awareness upon abhyasa as well as disinterestedness or vairagya for every other thought or form during meditation.

Abhyasa and vairagya will be established by sincerity and truth. You have to perfect abhyasa and vairagya. When perfected, a union will take place, then success in samadhi.

Be above physical slavery. Be above physical recreations. Never seek happiness from any man, matter or event. Seek it from within.

Be above physical stimulus and objective gain. Absolute freedom from mental conflicts, passions, etc. is possible if only one is aware of the real nature of world rooted in selfishness or khud garzi.

In order to serve society and maintain order, let one offer one's physical talents but spare the spirit and save the soul from eternal tortures inflicted by these self-esteemed worldlings. So be up, divine child, for realization!

Delhi, June 30, 1959

Let the inner lamp grow brighter and brighter. Let old leaves wither away. Let clouds subside. Let the great light prevail. Let divine forces rejoice in thee.

Then a day will come when the inner frame of your mind, which is the perceptual medium of all experiences, will be converted in the pattern of thy master. It is then that you will see him everywhere.

At present your thoughts, emotions and other mental attitudes are becoming fused in his remembrance. Your mind is in constant awareness with him. This is what we know as mental awareness.

Beyond the realm of this mental awareness, you will come upon the field of conscious visions. It is the plane of spirit. It is the plane of devas, so to say. Philosophers call it supramental awareness. It is here that the real process of

43

atma anubhuti starts. However, supramental awareness is not the ultimate awareness. You should not misunderstand supramental awareness for self-realization.

External thought currents are introverted in the beginning through pratyahara. Then those currents are focused through dharana. Then this concentrated current is reformed in the form of paramatman. When the process of this reformation is complete, when current is no more a current, there remains shuddha paramatman.

Prayers and bhajans will engage the emotions. Japa will introvert the tendencies. Concentration will assemble the scattered forms into one form of the master. Meditation will represent the form to the *form* itself.

Bhakti intensifies the process, deepens the awareness and protects the sadhaka from laziness as well as mental dissipation. The deeper the love, the more intense the awareness. Intense awareness helps in freeing oneself from mental drifting during sadhana. If there are fluctuations during sadhana, it only means that the awareness is not intense and love not constant.

So long as a sadhaka gives expression to 'street emotions', let me say, he has no settled frame of mind. Then what? He has to revise his personality. The yoga sadhaka should have such a strong and unshakeable mind that it will not even feel for death or any chaos. He must be a person of steady wisdom, sublimated emotions, right perception and realization. He must be a person of resolute will.

Another truth! Perfected love is realization. If only a sadhaka has perfect love for his Ishtam, he will find no delay in realizing him. He doesn't succeed just because his devotion has not become perfect as yet. He doesn't succeed just because a few adversities break the peace and serenity of his soul. He doesn't succeed just because insignificant and airy distractions came in the way of his mental equilibrium. He doesn't succeed just because he barters the peace of his mind for castles in the air. He doesn't succeed just because love and hatred, union and separation still have some

44

meaning for him. Yes, he fails just because he fails to retain the edifice of success.

This is a precious note. This is for deep, serious and sincere assimilation. Ego stands in your way to truth. Ego dies when meditation is born. Ego dies when bhakti is in her full bloom. Ego dies when awareness becomes overwhelming. Out of the death of ego is born darshan. Out of the death of ego is born atma anubhuti. Out of the death of ego is born aparoksha jnana.

Kill this ego and tensions will leave the jiva. Strenuousness will depart. Cravings for pleasuresome experiences will dwindle into nothing. Idleness will dissipate.

Then the light will be switched on. Then the light will be switched off. Then the light will shine all over. Then the light will be extinguished. Then the light will emerge. Then the light will get merged. Sages call it moksha and nirvana.

Know this truth another way. When awareness of God dawns, the awareness of the rest dies. When self-awareness stretches itself to every side of experience, the sense awareness ceases to function. Samadhi is the consummation of all vrittis in one supreme awareness.

Bandha Bazaar, July 26, 1959

So long as one depends upon external devices, internal success is impossible to attain. This is the nature of the mind. Therefore, the mind is to be snatched from its last device and resource. It is only then that it will invent an internal device. Necessity is the mother of invention. Necessity must be created. Does God, who does not respond to our call for life after life, forget us? Even so, I am trying to train your mind by occasional and abrupt silence. Indeed this is so that you might be forced to shake off the mental inertia which overpowers sadhakas from time to time.

The heart which God has given should be given to one, the ideal. When it is given to desires, passions and sense

45

pleasures, it causes restlessness and dissipation. And when the same heart is given to a great ideal – union with the self in samadhi or self-realization – it experiences peace, attains power, perceives light and gains wisdom.

By heart, I don't mean the biological stuff. It is what we are. It is a psychological stuff, which has a tendency to love and hate. It is always in need of someone upon which it could rest. When given to corrupt associations, it produces longing and clinging, frustration and insanity. When you utilize it for sadhana, it becomes a link between divine and human, supra-sensuous and sense experiences.

Indeed, the heart is to be absorbed by the thought of *one self*; it is there that it should abide. Love, which is an expression of heart, should be made to flow towards one who can consume it without getting agitated, like an ocean which consumes all rivers and yet remains undisturbed.

If any mental activity, say, love or hatred, disturbs or makes the heart restless, or excites more longings, it is shallow and narrow and miserly; for it could not consume either love or hatred. One who has consumed them remains undisturbed and unruffled either by love or hatred.

Since divine vision illumines one's inner life, and since the self abides in the inner altar, it is necessary to render the inner condition smooth, clear, balanced and happy. So the heart is to be united, love is to be consumed, and the personality must become free from psychological taints and strains with the help of regular and proper understanding without any bias, prejudice and reservation.

Buddhi or understanding will tell you that inner relation with sensual objects will disturb the tempo of meditation and cause delay in the attainment of samadhi. So what an intelligent sadhaka should do is this: he must give his heart in toto to one ideal. Then alone will the strains of daily life not interfere in meditation.

All other longings, except the desire to attain divine realization, lead to mental distortion. They are born of *ajnana*. Only the desire to see him face to face in his divine essence is helpful to a sadhaka.

46

Senses are turbulent. No use curbing them. They revive like the ten heads of Ravana. They mislead the mind. God-given good understanding alone can drive away the senses and control them with the help of the mind.

Emotions make the senses unruly. Sensitivity causes the mind to miss accurate judgement. Brooding destroys hard-earned self-confidence. Hatred pollutes the inner temple. Passions of all kinds persuade the jiva to undertake indiscriminate and feverish actions. Blessed be that man who has turned his gaze, withdrawn his senses, dedicated his heart and started dhyana!

Your japa anushthana is going on all right. Soon after the anushthana, again switch to the practice of concentration and meditation. A great deal of your sadhana should be finished before the dawn of summer. During the monsoon and winter seasons is the best time to remain enwrapped in his sumiran. Less strain is felt during rains and winter.

Experiment periodically on the condition of your willpower and receptivity of the astral system by punctually getting up in the morning at a fixed hour. Please remember that there should be no disturbance in sleep before the appointed hours.

Ajapa japa is internal continuity of nama sumiran, i.e. remembrance of the divine name. It is not felt when one is engrossed in certain absorbing thought or work. No sooner is the work or thinking over, it at once floats on the conscious surface, and you remember it. It not only gives serenity, but it changes facial expressions also by an addition of magnetism. It removes shyness and nervousness of mind and speech completely. The effects of ajapa japa, supramental sumiran, are reflected in reorientated behaviour expressing efficiency, goodness, purity, mastery over others, self-control and impressiveness. Still deeper in the inner chambers repairs, replacements, reshuffling and regeneration of all the inner parts of our machinery take place.

All this is not seen. However, one feels that some change for the better is taking place. One change is certain. As and when the ajapa japa goes on progressing, one strongly feels that all sorts of unnecessary thoughts which were hovering over the mind without effort and notice or inclination have ceased to a considerable extent. One feels, when one surveys the practice, that one was not thinking at all. This is because ajapa japa withdraws unto itself a lot of intramental activities which were going to waste without having any motive behind them.

At present, the tendency of the mind is to keep on thinking, to slip from one thought to another unnoticed, and maintain an active form by roaming either in the past or the present, so on and so forth. But progress in ajapa japa will have a strong hold over the mind and its tendencies. It will effect economy of thought. It will allow the mind to function where necessary. It will allow the mind to run from groove to groove without any purposeful aim. Apart from all this, supramental awareness will empty the subtle body of those contents which pollute it, and through it, purify the whole life. In short, ajapa japa is that stage of the jiva when the conscious mind is left free, while the inner mind does the japa.

So far as daily duties are concerned, you have to perform them. It is always better to work than to renounce. If it were not so, saints would have never worked after achieving jnana. It is not by the total renunciation of karmas that one attains jnana; in fact it is just the opposite. That is, one has to work in perfect awareness with the fullest ability at one's command. The three gunas of prakriti will compel him to act elsewhere, even if he renounces this present work.

Work would become a source of happiness if the spirit can recognize it as a stepping-stone towards the path of samadhi.

Do you work merely for the physical needs of life? No. Karma is an outlet for our mixed samskaras; karma perfects our soul. It is a yoga or a method of self-control.

After the attainment of samadhi, one can, of course, do as one likes. Presently, the tendency of the mind is to waver.

So it does not relish a particular work. Well, renounce the work, but you will find it wavering again for this or that work. So it is a tendency of asthira manas to crave for a departure from present circumstances. The sadhaka has to judge his mind carefully, whether it wants a change for better vistas, or just wavers.

This world, a product of sense consciousness, is very true and solid for one whose consciousness has not transcended the boundaries of sense experience.

This world is dead to a jnani who has reached the supra-sensuous stage. And the supra-sensuous stage is hardly believed by one who is engrossed in the world of the senses. It is an unreality to him. And this stage of samadhi is the only reality for a sage who is living in it. So you have two things: sense consciousness and self-awareness. A sage is unaware of sense consciousness. A jiva is unaware of self-awareness.

Vairagya intensifies sadhana. It give good results. Sadhana becomes qualitative.

> Ye, transcend sorrow and misery!
> I am ringing you up,
> But where have you gone?
> To attend the feast of Indriyas?
> Thy Soul is forever with me; I with you.
> We talk of higher things;
> And not of body, which is not all-pervading.
> Thy Soul and my Soul,
> Though separated by time and space, are one.
> Not that you have to join the two in ONE;
> Just rend asunder the separating factors
> By understanding and sadhana.
> And when the wall is gone and the veil removed,
> You shall forget who was who.
> For the river would have become Ocean.

49

'Jagte Raho!' Be eternally aware of thy atma – the all-pervading consciousness. He will come at any time. Close the doors and windows and ventilators and every other passage. Now, none knows, none sees.

The real bliss of yoga is felt in a closed chamber! One can't commune on pavements. Yoga needs seclusion, exclusiveness, no disturbance and privacy. It is then that the fullest satisfaction can be experienced. Let one understand that the sense doors should be closed by drawing the mind unto him. It can be done anywhere.

The greatest obstacle in meditation is the revival of sense experiences or the relational experiences. Even the most insignificant experiences or perceptions float to the surface during concentration and slow down the process.

Even if all other sense experiences are controlled, the sweet experience of physical bliss somehow remains unconquered.

Among all impressions, the impression of sex contact is long-lasting. He who has become unmindful of its impressions and past experiences has come closer to the ultimate success.

The experiences of sexual touch, emotion, contact, etc. disturb the theme or tempo of concentration. It is only after the least idea of sex is fried in the spiritual fire of vairagya that meditation culminates in samadhi!

Aged persons are disturbed by pleasant and unpleasant memories and various experiences of the past, while youngsters are disturbed more by longings than by memories of the past.

Until one attains intellectual and sexual maturity, there invariably exist suppressed emotions wanting expression. We may not notice them on our conscious plane; that is another thing. Nevertheless, clinging or desire for yet unattained pleasures does exist. As soon as one is amidst favourable conditions for fulfilment, one has them with all pleasure.

So long as there is any longing hidden even in the remotest corner of the mind, there is every chance of its finding favourable circumstances for fulfilment. But he who

50

has still greater desire for samadhi is almost free from the demands of that longing.

All other desires are but forms of a single desire, 'to love and be loved'. In other words, there is a tendency in everybody to seek oneness, and establish union.

We have keenly observed that the efforts of the jiva to merge in atma are reflected in his futile attempts to love the world and be loved by it. It is only when it fails in loving and being loved by this world that it *seeks* the union in its own self.

You like the one who loves you, because you think that his consciousness has assimilated your consciousness. You don't like the one who criticizes you, because you think that his consciousness is setting aside your consciousness.

The fact is this: we like unity, merger, dedication, inseparability, self-surrender and non-duality. This is the law governing all our behaviours.

Unfortunately, what happens, do you know? We experiment with this law wherever possible, only to realize in the end it was not a real union, a real oneness.

Tired of all petty experiments, we turn to our own self and begin to love it. We see within us all that there is in the world; and something more also. We see within us an eternal master, an ever aware witness, a non-dual companion and a true lover. There we surrender ourselves.

And this self is projected in friends, wife, children and all the rest. And this very self is objectified in all names and forms where we had so far attempted to seek love and communion. But this self is projected more gloriously in saints, gurus and noble men. And when this jiva seeks unity with them, it finds it; yes, it does find union.

Unto him is unfolded this union, who has transcended past impressions, whether sweet or bitter. Unto him this self reveals itself, who has gone far beyond the recapitulations of the sweetest sense pleasures. He alone whom no event of the past can influence, no anxiety and anticipation of the future grab and no reflection of previous lives impress sees the self in all its glory.

51

Yogis come to know all about their lives, all about others, yet they live like simple souls, unmindful of anything, and resting in their own self.

There was a prince who played the part of a dhobi. He didn't play it well, for he couldn't adjust. Another prince played the part of a dhobi and he played it well, for he thought he should just bow down to the work and work with the stream of life which surrounds us – and like this we must remember our nature, while playing as jiva marvellously; for we are consciousness absolute.

Bandha Bazaar, August 7, 1959

Atman is the expression of beyond – yes, beyond the senses of sound, touch, taste and smell, beyond thought, intelligence, memory and feeling. Far beyond the experiences of this body, mind and empirical existence, at the height of perfect silence and oneness, there is *someone* whom yogis have seen in the superconscious state. That is atman.

After transcending the earthly consciousness, yogis commune with him who is immortal – whose body is all that you see and who is the essence of everything. He is rasa – the blissful taste of love. Upon attaining him, one becomes bliss itself.

He alone who has united in Godly love no vishayananda can affect, no spring tide can upset, and no flesh can attract.

As soon as he is seen, all other perceptions vanish like nightmares. Having seen him in deep silence, values change; the world has a different meaning. When you bring the light, the darkness is removed; the path is illumined. Know this from me, that *the path remains*; darkness alone disappears.

Truly has it been said that at the dawn of jnana, the world is no more. That is to say, your preconceived values born of maya, moha, mamata, kama, etc. are annihilated in the wake of sage-consciousness.

52

For an ajnani, passion, anger, greed, etc. make the world which, after attaining jnana, disappear in toto. The world of maya, moha, mamata, ahamkara and all other illusory values is dead to a sage. He is alive to that world which is atma maya. He is conscious of a new world of absolute values. It is there that he disseminates knowledge.

'Mr X is dead to me' means that I have shifted my attachment from him. 'For Sri Sukadeva, there were no women in this world' means that he had disidentified his self and that his valuation of sex was rooted in absolute self-hood – atma eva idam sarvam.

'World' is not only an aggregate of physical elements, such as life, etc. Money is not the world; it is our attitude to it which creates world or worldliness. Death is not the world; it is our attachment for one who is dead which really fashions this world. So did I truly say that the world of raga-dwesha and other similar conflicts is dead for a sage.

Regarding sounds: you need not even produce any sound, as you are doing at present. Just close the ears and eyes. Try to listen to subtle sounds in the right ear.

In the right is the channel of pingala nadi or surya nadi. At times you will hear through the left ear also. Ida nadi or chandra nadi flows in the left. These two join at the confluence heading for sahasrara when meditation merges in samadhi. Try to hear through the right ear.

In this practice of nada anusandhana, you will have to penetrate through the subtle sounds, which can be traced with non-dual practices of inner observation. These sounds can be heard even without uttering any audible sound which you where asked to produce in the beginning. Of course, that will need a keen sense of concentrated observation. You will hear those inner sounds by gradual practice.

The first sound is like the song of separation of a nightingale; sometimes in quick succession and sometimes in a prolonged rhythm.

The second sound is that of a silver bell, which at once brings a vision of a starry night.

The third is as if someone is producing musical notes from a great distance. It is a feminine voice, shrill and thinned out.

The fourth is a veena. The fifth is a flute. The sixth is a drum. The seventh, which is the last one, is the roaring of clouds, ultimately ending with the falling of a thunderbolt as if it were at a remote distance. With this, the sadhaka is *inside*.

These are the seven principle sounds. Some sadhakas hear three more sounds, which are a conch, clapping and a mridanga.

A bhakta attains bhava samadhi. A yogi attains nirvikalpa. A hatha yogi attains jada samadhi. A jnani attains prajna. All these samadhis lead to jivanmukti in their own way.

It is good that you are participating in household duties. That will give you sufficient inner strength necessary for meditation.

When you are totally absorbed in your office work, don't think of diversions of any kind – not even external awareness. By gradual practice your inner body will adjust all affairs in due course. Your entire external being will be absorbed in karma. At the same time, somewhere deep in you awareness will continue. it must be spontaneous. Don't get confused by many diversions.

One work at one time. Total absorption in any work will gradually train the mind to forget its usual fickleness and unsteady character. If you plunge into any work at hand with non-dual keenness and attention, you will only derive immense help in meditation.

The main obstacle in meditation is the mind's old habit of delving into matters related to past, future and so on. Absorbing yourself in karmas ruthlessly break this old habit of mind, so the mind becomes fit for meditation.

You are asked to practise sumiran only during leisure, especially when the mind is not required to be totally attentive. Any work which requires the whole of your attention trains the mind in steadiness. Karma yoga is a stage of preparation of mind for yoga and meditation. Soon after an absorbing duty is over, bring him up in your consciousness. You will be surprised at your success.

The main work remains to be done. You have to empty the vessel of its various contents. 'Empty thyself', said Jesus Christ. It is the same yoga by which you empty your consciousness of its various vrittis – thought waves.

When the consciousness would be saturated in his awareness; when the ideal, ambition, reflection, love, anticipation, hatred, action, rest and all movements would be diverted for his cause; when rain and thunder, winter and chill, night and wilderness, birth and death, praise and insult, would lose their effects in the wake of overwhelming awareness of *one*; when Bilwamangal would become unmindful of torrents, jungles, thorns, the overflooded river, the dead body and the hanging snake for his Chintamani, for her love and in her constant awareness – it is then, verily then, that the vessel would really become empty of its confusing contents.

Indeed, in this vessel alone would the highest purity prevail, indomitable courage abide and all the powers of nature flourish. If you have in you that one-pointed awareness of form, then you are really blessed.

You are still under the wrong conception that your guru is geographically and physically far from you. He is in you. Between you and him is just a veil; a veil of meditational incapacity and lack of spiritual vision. This is the distance. Open the door, just step in and look within. Don't look back; yes, on and on, in and in.

There in your fourth chamber he dwells. The pathway to his palace is sadhana. The zeal to reach the palace is bhakti. The key to open the lock is concentration. The attempt to enter in is pratyahara. The transcendence of three chambers is meditation and the fourth chamber is where he is.

There the two become ONE. There the long-awaited union. There the 'end all' of all dual efforts. There one can't

55

think through the mind, can't see with the eyes, can't perceive through sense experiences. The intellect can't function there, much less speech.

In that chamber long-forgotten glory shines. Eternal light! Shiva and Shakti merge there in each other. Names and forms vanish. That is the ultimate goal of divine love – bhakti. That is the abode of truth. That is the abode of thy guru.

Your guru will come when the rains in thy life would have passed away. He will come when the night would be perfectly silent. He will come when you would be all alone, *none in thee*. Surely he will rise from within yourself like a sunbeam – sudden, unwarranted and awe-inspiring.

He will neither come in dreams, nor in waking, nor even in sleep, not at all in thoughts. When thy kith and kin, lifelong companions and old relatives (samskaras and worldly consciousness) would have gone into dead slumber, it is then that he will descend from the heights just to take you up with him. Let the night come and the world sleep; let there be none in his way. He will certainly come upon thy soul. Note the time and place.

Prior to his arrival! A nightingale will sing aloud; a silver bell will ring under starry skies, an angel will sing from the ocean; a veena will be harped upon, drums will be beaten; a flute will be played; and with the falling of a thunderbolt he will descend upon thee.

Prior to his arrival! Lights of various colours will flash in the sky; someone will secretly visit thee; fire will pass through thee; angels will appear; fierce spirits will come to inform thee about his arrival; and someone will come and lift thee up in the air; and with the appearance of a host of overwhelming clouds of different hues, he will arise from thee. *He will come* when the place is ready for him.

56

No one who has experienced meditation will be attracted by the pull of maya. No one who has experienced meditation will be lost in the whirlpool of desires and passion.

The senses can't see the chamber of meditation. Experiences of meditation are undying. Pure reason alone can peep into that chamber. No wise man will like to renounce meditation.

The eyes see diversity. The ears hear diverse sounds. Similarly so do the other senses. Not so in dhyana. Because the senses can't exist in meditation. Then who to see and whom? Who to talk and with whom?

Even as various clothes are known as nothing but cotton, even as various houses are known as nothing but mud, even as various ornaments are known as nothing but gold, likewise all are seen in the atma.

Even as an intoxicated man also discharges his duties, even as a mother engaged with her baby doesn't miss her duties, likewise a dhyana yogi works; of course, the spirit is different. A crow might fly anywhere; let him. However, let him not lose sight of his only support.

Even as storms disturb the ocean, winds disturb the lakes, abuse disturbs the mind, quarrels disturb the peace, so do the senses disturb the mind.

Even as a snake charmer tames snakes, so do you tame the mind. Mantra is a tamer. Herbs are tamers. Weapons are tamers. All of them fail to tame the mind. Love of God is the last, fastest and best and the only tamer of mind.

So I have given you a few glimpses of that ananda which is born of dhyana, and which you had asked for.

Take mental rest. Remain a witness. However, don't be a pessimist. Throw away the self-styled yokes of worry and anxiety. Everything takes its own course. In fact, divine law operates uniformly over all. Perfect mental peace is a life rejuvenator.

Live is a divine sport, let us play it accordingly. Life is a wonderful display of sorrow and elation. When everything has been said, then life is nothing but a product of our own mind. Merge the mind in its source. This is the way to real happiness.

There is a garden with flower plants in it; again, honey-bees on them. All beauty and all grace. Lo, the gardener sees the beauties fading and flowers falling. He hurries to collect the valuable seeds. Let one meditate on this.

Remember that impurity in vital consciousness is a great barrier on the path of success.

Ideas pertaining to sex will never let one rest in peace. Worldly love and divine love can't coexist. All arguments of mind are invalid and useless. Mental equilibrium is of primary importance. Courage, courage and courage! Do not invite fears. Do your duty. Be bold and adjust; but not to the extent of self-distortion.

Vairagya is a false notion. It is self-deception. Love is real. Love your Ishtam. This alone is positive vairagya.

Let your Ishta Devata come true in your visions; then only can you say that you have faith in him. Until then your faith is unconsciously divided, in spite of your assertion, "I have faith in him."

You will have success. Be stronger still. Reorganize your vital consciousness, so that you may see purity in yourself as well as everywhere. No amount of resolves will substantially help you to maintain purity, unless you have reorganized your inner soul.

Be aware, you are a bird; there are hunters. Guru is a note of caution.

Do send me your monthly report of sadhana at once. I am more particular about your progress rather than your reverential thanks. My exclusive interest in you is spiritual enlightenment. That's all.

Rajnandgaon, December 25, 1959

You see, I don't like emotional programs. I like serious and deep and pukka thinking. It doesn't matter whether you succeed or not, but you have to work up your spiritual practices gradually, naturally and yet sincerely. Real success comes when off-handed operations completely cease. Don't you feel that this bit of progress you have so far made takes years and years for many others to achieve? You may not realize; but I know it too well. There are those sadhakas also who have not even that much success.

Well, I am your kind mother. True. You can open your sinful heart to me. Allowed. But don't you think that such thoughts only interfere in spiritual progress? Spiritual progress demands a serene, cool, calm and thick-skinned mental condition. You might have expressed all that in a spirit of 'apnapan'; but don't you feel that such expressions only disturb the inner frame and mental base? How many times should I tell you to maintain mental equilibrium? *Are bhai* – equibalanced mind is the ground for mystic visions.

Don't you know that the purest and noblest of persons too have been criticized and slandered? Let me say that every man has been a target of criticism and scandals. To be receptive towards them is to invite unhappiness. "Let them say what they say" is an old adage.

On the other hand, if you are noble, you must turn a deaf ear to all remarks. How can a pure man feel for impure allegations? Those who are influenced only prove that they have black spots on themselves. Please understand this truth

59

before you jump up to say, "When a holy man finds himself falsely alleged, he feels great hurt." Oh no! A holy man is as adamant and enduring as a mountain.

Still you need to strengthen your faith. Please don't think that you have perfected it. The day it is perfectly perfected you will acquire power. I quite agree with you that faith does not become perfect in a single day. I am only reminding you.

Concentration should be done on that concrete form which is easy to conceptualize. If one can concentrate well on the abstract mental form, well and good. A photo is required only if the mental form is difficult to conceptualize. If one finds it difficult to visualize him mentally, then a photo should help. Whenever the mental image of the Ishta vanishes, a photo will help to regain it. In the beginning the photo alone is helpful. But gradually one should attempt mental dharana.

One can talk to that inner form. But always remember that the mental picture should be presented in one and the same posture. Don't change it when once a particular posture has been decided. The idea is that the form one has chosen must continue as a definite posture, colour, dress, height, etc. up to the last. If any other form tries to replace that chosen one during meditation, it will only upset the inner pattern of the mind. So one has to decide once and for all as to which form he likes to meditate upon. Say, if he has decided upon the form of his Ishta seated in a meditative posture, then let him meditate upon that alone. If it is difficult and strenuous, then let him be contented with the photo alone.

The yoga sadhaka has to feel as if the Ishta is sitting in front of him in a meditative posture; this is one form of dharana. Or else let him see him as standing and blessing the sadhaka in all kindness; this is another form of dharana. If nothing of this sort is possible, then trataka on the photo will have to be practised at first in order to collect the mental energies. When this process is complete, then only should he go in for dharana or mental visualization. Ultimately it is the *mental picture* which will pave the way for dhyana.

You will have to note down the experiences. It will reveal unto you those experiences which you had during meditation, and which you had forgotten later on in the wake of sense consciousness. What happens actually is that a neophyte forgets all the experiences of meditation when he comes back to the plane of sense consciousness. If you make it a point to exert yourself at writing down the experiences, you will invent a technique of remembering those dormant experiences. You may not be able to do it so well in the beginning; however, gradually you will do it successfully. You will have to pen the process of meditation, phase by phase, about the form, its colour, disappearance, so on and so forth.

Now you have to understand one more fact very well. From now onwards you will have to observe passionlessness in (a) thought, (b) word and (c) practice. Brahmacharya means mental freedom, verbal freedom and sexual freedom from the consciousness of the opposite sex. At this stage of yogic practices if brahmacharya is not observed, you will not only utterly fail, you will ruin your mind as well. Cases of such errors are too many to be quoted here. I tell you all this with great emphasis. This sadhana will have to be given proper attention from now onwards. He who can't maintain brahmacharya should remain satisfied with a little puja path. He should never appear for higher meditation.

Sex conscious bachelors would derive more harm than benefit from higher dhyana yoga. Sex conflicts in a bachelor, added to keen concentration, damage the brain mechanism, not to speak of what happens if they indulge in cinema, non-vegetarianism, novels and similar other nerve-weakening activities. You know all this very well. Yet, I should repeat the 'signal' from time to time.

Talk only when necessary. Don't keep on parroting unnecessarily. After a little observation, you will know more about it. At this spiritual stage useless talking will retard

61

your progress. Make it a point to talk to the point. Simplify your answers. I don't mean that you should spoil affairs by not talking. What I am aiming at is 'essential talking'. This will not only minimize verbal commitments, it will help you in your meditation as well. This much about verbal regulation.

Observe mouna on Sundays as well as on other holidays. Mouna should be observed in the form of sadhana and swadhyaya.

Now, about mental silence. This is really very important. Mental silence is not what they call 'not thinking'. Mental silence is really a positive state, when the sadhaka is either remembering the name or the form instead of all and sundry things. Even thoughts of the body should not come to the mind, except the name and the feelings of his presence and divinity. Practise this mental silence in the form of japa, sumiran and swadhyaya. This will bestow mental strength as well as psychological diversion. Instead of seeing your Ishtam perceptibly in all men and women, which is nothing but foolishness, you should fuse the mind in a central form and feelings. I mean yaad, remembrance.

You think too fast and too many things. Don't you know that they only weaken the faculties of meditation? Can't you silence thinking and brooding? You can't run away from evil. Evil is everywhere.

Be bold, hero! Where is the knot of ashanti? What is that bondage which you want me to cut? Should I tell you that the knot is thy mind? Sannyasa will not solve the problems; that will only tighten the knot. What do you mean by 'to set out for the search of truth'? Have I not told you that one need not at all stir out in search of truth? It can be searched for anywhere. True it is that after having known the truth, one has to stir out to proclaim that unto all. But how can you proclaim unless you know it? How can you know it unless you have realized it through intuition? No amount of bookish and verbal knowledge will reveal the truth unto thee. Dharana, then dhyana and then samadhi!

62

You should rather feel restlessness for not having realized this truth. Efforts should be made to convert the subtlest and nirakara truth into conscious and sakara truth. Repeated sadhana and unflinching faith will help you to realize the truth face to face. And again, this truth in you and that truth elsewhere are one and the same. You will realize *this truth* first; then, through this truth you will know *that truth*. This truth is atma; that truth is paramatma.

Side by side stabilize mental serenity. Nothing should disturb your inner ananda. The only thing one can do is to abuse you or insult you. Oh, all these are mental vibrations! If you lend your ears, you are doomed. Laugh them away, and you are saved. So worry not, hurry not and puzzle not.

Rajnandgaon, December 13, 1959

Within this short period a great change has taken place. This change should have been brought about earlier if you had surrendered your ego. Now of course your ego remains surrendered. All this should bring home to you that perfect, unreserved and wholesale surrender of egocentricity is the key to unlocking the hidden gates of sadhana and divinity.

There is something in you which you will realize as '*I am That*'. Based upon this unseen truth, I have been convincing you that you can see your Ishta everywhere. You can even talk to him. Constant awareness and remembrance are fanning the fire of your faith.

Why do you wonder at the temporary vairagya which people develop for some time and which fades away very soon? It's because there is no one to help them to maintain spiritual equilibrium. It is not a matter of pity. It is a lesson to be learned. This is how the mind behaves until it has been surrendered and cast into a pattern. From time to time the divine in them attempts to express itself in the form of good thoughts. But again, in the absence of permanent stimuli, it is eclipsed by maya, which comes in the form of environmental influences. One should have living faith in higher things. One should be aware of evil propensities. It is only then that one can maintain a higher degree of divine nature. One should have an aim. This is a very important aid in keeping the awareness of vairagya alive.

The moment one loses faith and forgets the aim, one succumbs to anger, jealousy, etc. It is these forces which destroy the patterns of one's mental energy by introducing fears and conflicts. So long as one has in him passion, anger, greed, delusion, fear, jealousy and egoism, he will not be able to exercise his divine will. Again, so long as he has no guru, no mantra, no aim, no faith and no love, he will not be able to do away with these dark forces. The secret of your success is that you have dedicated yourself. The reason for worldly people's failure is that they are like logs of wood, tossing hither and thither, amidst a great ocean of problems, etc.

You are progressing. You are heading towards balance. You are becoming 'clear-minded'. Your divine force is rejoicing, because you have cleared its path of pilgrimage to a very great extent. Be calm; don't at all attempt to exercise your atma shakti. The time is coming when your mere presence will heal the sick, comfort the unfortunate, bless the seekers and guide the sadhaka. Veil after veil has been rent asunder. Clouds have been destroyed. The next work due is the materialization of form in meditation, in dream and *at will*. Materialization in dreams first, in deep meditation next and then by willing.

Don't exercise your atma shakti at all. If at all you do, exercise it for non-strenuous concentration and materialization. Exercise it by all means for your spiritual progress. Utilize it to render your mind calm and cool. Exercise it to improve your life in general. Exercise it in order to wake you up at will. Sometimes at 4.09 a.m., sometimes at 4.15 a.m., sometimes at 3.59 a.m. Thus you will be able to gauge its power, efficacy and success. The best thing is to take the help of your atma shakti for success in sadhana only.

Wear saris decently. Renounce silken dresses if you are using them at all. Gives up the use of cosmetics. Inner beauty is imperishable. Inner beauty is magnetic. Inner beauty is born of purity, devotion, faith, dharma and samadhi. Inner beauty radiates peace, consolation, comfort, cure and blessings. Inner beauty is real, everlasting and priceless.

Sleep on your left. Sit in vajrasana regularly. Start your day with japa and sumiran and close it in the same spirit. Sleep well; rest in him. Soon after your sadhana, palm your eyes; you will be able to do away with your glasses forever. Intently gazing at the photo will revive your optic nerve capacity. But don't overdo the practice in the beginning.

New Year is coming. Remain intoxicated in his consciousness at every stage of life. May not the ever-changing scenes of the world disturb you! Face the storms and earthquakes! Don't be shocked; don't fall down. Keep on standing majestically.

Ahmedabad, March 2, 1960

You can take tea after bathing and asanas; but it is always good to give up this habit. If you can't, then you can have a cup at about 6.30 a.m. Milk at about 8 a.m.

Mind plays havoc. It advances lame excuses. It creates many obstacles. One has to tackle the mind tactfully. Control of habits plays a very prominent role during the initial stages of sadhana. A sadhaka should have a fuller understanding of the mind and its habits.

The seed of samadhi is already in you. You will be able to develop the seed into a full-fledged tree by gradual meditation.

My soul expands in the morning as well as at night towards my children. Those who are (a) empty, (b) receptive and (c) qualified can receive those spiritual currents and become merged in the overwhelming flood of consciousness.

Those who practise it day by day will get surprising results on any fine day. They will be possessed by that super-subtle consciousness. During this period, when they are occupied by this spirit of truth, they will act marvellously and express wonderful versatility.

Even now, it is possible for you to receive me within you. However, more purification must efface your individual ego and other similar traits, so that this event becomes permanent and useful.

Insofar as your extrovert mind is concerned, it is wholly occupied by his awareness. Your astral body is being occupied wholly by the practice of nama smaran. In due course, every atom of your outer and inner life will become a fit altar for the descent of and occupation by the spirit of truth.

Day by day the inner light must grow more and more effulgent. The outer lights must be controlled by the inner switch, so that he might come to you and occupy you and exhibit his lilas through you.

Does the mind still feel lazy? Are you still 'not very serious' about your single aim? Don't you have that much love and devotion in you that you could get entry into the inner chamber?

How does a child feel for his mother in her absence as well as in her presence? Likewise you must awaken the dormant prem and bhakti. Lukewarm prem will not do. Overwhelming, overpowering and intoxicating love is the secret. Like Chaitanya, Mira and Radha. Shake off the inner lethargy! Awaken your devoted and loving soul!

Padmasana. By and by you will be able to retain it for hours together. Also remember uddiyana, sirshasana, mayurasana and jala neti, as well as the twelve mantras of surya namaskara.

Practise pranayama along with kumbhaka. Keep the windows open during the practice. Don't overdo bhastrika, kapalbhati, sheetali and sheetkari; just a few rounds each and every day.

Never give up remembering, admiring and recognizing others' importance. This will purify your vyavaharic mind.

Never, never and never criticize. Do not at all lose your temper. Do not boast about yourself. Talk of sadhana only

66

to those who are really desirous to know about it. Talk very little, to the point, with perfect precision, effect and confidence.

Ahmedabad, March 5, 1960

Detach, detach. You are a soul of heaven. Nothing can touch you. You are beyond joy and sorrow. Do not identify yourself with success and failure. Your duty is to work. God does everything for good.

What do you mean by problems? You are the clue to all problems. Every problem will be solved by you alone. God is always in thee to guide you. Intelligent people don't expose their wealth to anybody. This is the way to keep wealth safe. The world is ready to exploit us and take our earnings and savings. Intelligent persons should be on guard, one can't believe anyone. Seths don't disclose their accounts. Do you understand? *Siddhi is the secret wealth.*

For the man of God, past, present and future are alike. For the man of the soil, the past is laden with repentance, the present with dissatisfaction, the future with anticipation. Who are you?

Stop thinking. Act. Merely act. Don't view an exaggerated form of events.

Rajnandgaon, March 21, 1960

Your ideas regarding seclusion. I am fully aware that a certain part of sadhana will have to be done only in seclusion. However, it goes without saying that domestic responsibilities give you a chance to cultivate patience, forbearance and to develop a hippopotamic constitution. Unfavourable conditions pave the way to everlasting spiritual strength. It is only under adverse circumstances that the mind really becomes steady and strong.

67

I am aware that you are progressing. I am also conscious that your inner life is growing far more steady and discriminative than that of a sadhaka in the Himalayas.

Now you need eternal strength of mind to maintain the gifts of concentration. Concentration, along with its gifts, is destroyed in a second if one lacks mental strength and allows the mind to dissipate in raga and dwesha.

Anticipation of the future create obstacles in the spiritual path. Let him do as he likes. You have to keep your mind free from disturbing thoughts of past and future. Such thoughts will not only kill the powers of will and consciousness, they will also introduce dissatisfaction, repentance, fear and pessimism in your life.

Work for him. Be free from affectations. Thus your mind will never get disturbed by the pairs of opposites and repentance.

Live as a witness both of happiness and misery. Don't identify yourself with any sort of happening – be it good or bad. The joy of sadhana alone should give you satisfaction. No other kind of joy should take you off your heels, inasmuch as no sorrow should drag you down.

Success gives elation. Failure creates depression. This is the plight of worldly men. The sadhaka is neither puffed up by success, nor disappointed by failures. He considers himself as an impartial spectator of the tragedies and comedies of this drama of life.

Mental detachment will redouble the force of your sadhana. Try to practise impartial spectatorship. This will make your mind steady enough to receive and maintain the light of concentration.

Let the body live in the world. Let the mind rest in consciousness. Dedicate thy actions to him. Develop a spiritual smile within the recesses of your atma, experience immense joy and bliss within and without.

At this stage, when I am installing psychic links with you, your mind is wavering in the name of tyaga and vairagya. Beware! This is a trick of the mind. The mind is trying to

68

drag you away. How then can you expect success in the absence of mental steadiness? Has it not been said that inner steadiness is a prerequisite on the path of yoga?

Raigarh, April 13, 1960

Light is by thy side; light is within; beyond the darkness. World perception is darkness. Self-experience is light. Purity of mind is light. Serenity is light. Viveka is light. Sorrow is darkness. Worry is darkness. Jealousy is darkness.

Passion kills the soul. Thoughts of various kinds kill spiritual stamina. 'Stop thinking' is the 'Open Sesame' of Ali Baba. The less you think, the greater you become. Control the thoughts by various means of pratyahara and concentration, such as work, japa, smaran and sadhana.

Inner peace is dynamic. Sleep and lethargy do not represent inner peace. Once it is obtained, nothing can shake the soul. Having obtained inner peace, one becomes powerful.

Shake off alasya and pramad. Be up and doing. Speed up. Where is the accelerator? Control tamas by proper diet, bathe twice a day and practise spiritual zeal.

Raipur (Rewa), April 17, 1960

Spiritual life is not a matter for joking. Self-realization is not for fun. Yet it is the easiest of all tasks provided the sadhaka doesn't allow himself to be influenced by the effects of what is agreeable and disagreeable.

It is not only meditation which is responsible for self-realization; but it is mental status also which is as important as any other sadhana.

Whenever the mind loses the divine touch, it identifies itself with happiness and sorrow, thus becoming a victim of the three gunas.

69

Why after all do we lose our mental balance? Just because we become partners in all life's events; just because we become interested in all we come across; just because we have sufficient emotion in reserve for that which is worldly. In short, we lose balance only if we become one with worldly happenings.

Inner peace is of utmost importance. It is a pure state of mind. In this state the mind is of course active and alert, but does not act as a partner.

Inner peace is far beyond inertia. Sleep is not inner peace. Forgetfulness is not inner peace. Proper understanding is inner peace. Inner peace is not a state of unawareness of events; in fact, one can obtain it along with every knowledge of moments and events.

The path of sadhana is hard to walk upon. The path of the world is easier. The fruit of sadhana is eternal power. The fruit of the world is perpetual frustration. One is hard in the beginning; another is easier. The wise one chooses one of them, considering the fruits thereof. Sugar is sweet; but acts like acid. Neem is bitter, but kills poison.

However, worldly happiness is quick in bearing fruits. It is quite intelligible. It is easily attainable. It has charming landscapes and glamorous ups and downs. It is full of flowers and fragrance. It is blissful. Passion, greed and attachment are its magical chantings.

Spiritual life is long, strenuous, barren and fruitless at its very outset. It is a plunge into the unknown. Its rewards are beyond intelligence, therefore, uncertain. One has to strive, strive and strive – sometimes for lives and lives together. It needs constant vigilance and care. It is a mission fit for heroes. Cowards and timid people will find it terribly hard and hot. Bold and brave soldiers alone can undertake this mission. Emotional and passionate individuals will find it troublesome. After all, who can bear the rigors of vairagya?

But with all that has been said, it is an irrefutable fact that spiritual life alone is the ultimate destiny of all. And knowing thus, when we embrace spiritual life, we must keep

70

this fact before our mind; that activities are not to be given up and responsibilities are not to be shirked. An uphill task! Isn't it?

Actions and responsibilities do not bind the sadhaka who takes over the part of a witness. Actions and responsibilities do not bind the sadhaka if he doesn't identify himself with the effects of agreeable and disagreeable. One need not strive to give up duties. On the other hand, duties themselves leave a man when he becomes considerably free from samskaras.

This truth must open your eyes, my child! Your soul is taking flight. Let nothing interfere with its speed. Even a little ashanti will completely undo the great achievements you have made so far.

While living amidst all, yet living in the inner chamber, live thou in both the chambers. While talking to all, yet maintaining inner silence, talk thou in both the languages.

Shake off the dust of influences. Wash your mind of all the mental dirt in toto. Revive your zeal, aim and faith. Regain inner happiness. Dissociate mentally from both good and bad. Go on working physically as you have been instructed beforehand. Neither passion nor anger, neither sorrow nor pleasure should betray you. Your God is in you. He is in all. For him alone you work. For him you eat and live. This jnana should sustain your zeal, aim and faith.

Don't worry about the weight reduction. It is natural. Old toxic matter is going out. Finally new and pure matter will be added to your body. Take proper care of your diet. Roti, milk, saag, etc.

Summer is in the offing. Stop halasana. Minimize paschi-mottanasana. Stop bhastrika. Continue uddiyana. Sirshasana – ten to thirty seconds will do. Continue all other asanas. Take a bath twice daily in the morning and evening. Take milk also. Reduce or stop tea totally.

Ye sadhaka, don't care if no one gives you recognition. Don't strive after gaining importance. Don't at all worry what others say about you. Whether the world approves of you or not, don't waste time thinking rubbish, please!

71

Your letter of confession of your mental depressions and disturbance. I am so glad that you have at least judged yourself. Please take care of your mind and health. Mind and body sustain the soul. Constant work and mental engagement keep the inner instruments in order. Arguments and reflections weaken the mind. Feelings and opinions are detrimental to normal progress in life.

Meditation opens the gate. It links the mind with the past, present and future. It develops willpower and the power of personality. More about meditation is to be experienced personally.

Man lives in vain hopes. He doesn't perceive the will of the divine in the proper light. He wants to solve matters according to his own merji (wish) and prejudices. Why not obey the commands; for there alone lies happiness? Leave everything to be worked out by his mercy.

We want events to move according to our personal choice. So we suffer and repent and live a dead existence with frustration all throughout our life.

How easy and cheap and light it is to say, "I love God; I love guru." How hard is it to withstand the unpleasant tests. Still we crave for grace.

Let us, therefore, revise the chapter of our life thoroughly. Let us eliminate disturbing and horrible mistakes. It is never too late to rewrite history. We still have time to repair the car. There are still many chances for us to wake up, rise and realize the goal. Let us not become hopeless. Let us not lose courage. So long as there is life, let us revive it.

Amarkantak, June 21, 1960

Mental equilibrium is a preliminary process to sadhana. Divine grace descends upon those who have perfected mental poise.

The most difficult of all yogic practices is that practice wherein the aspirant realizes and sees his mysterious role behind all trials and discomforts.

Trials and tribulations are but the forms of his grace. They serve as a barometer to indicate the seriousness and grossness of imperfect personality. But for trying conditions, one couldn't gauge one's personality.

Samskaras of the past have to be fried up. Disease, discomfort, disturbance, insult, unpleasant situations; all these help one to purge foreign matter from the soul.

God creates every event with a great purpose behind it. Wise men don't oppose it,for they know his mission.

Know ye this truth very well; that praise and appreciation and love and recognition have only stood in the way of your spiritual progress. Still you crave for the same. What nonsense!

Fortunate was Christ who was crucified.

Fortunate were Socrates and Mansoor; what about Mira and Dayananda?

How unfortunate are we when we find ourselves allured by praise and favours, flowers and merits!

Misfortune unsurpassed! When trials come to our door, we cry out aloud to help us kick them away. Yea, we only kick divine chances. So do you understand!

Satyam feels his grace and mercy when tempests 'try to move him. Oh yes, Satyam thanks all of them because they come to judge and confirm his strength. You call them *shoes*; I call them *flowers*.

Flowers! Verily, they are the destroyers of my soul.

Abuse, insults, injuries, taunts, harassment, discomforts, etc. have strengthened my personality. Let me repeat my mantra, which my guru whispered into my soul:

> *Adapt, adjust, accommodate;*
> *Bear insult, bear injury; highest sadhana.*

Can you install and effect psychic communications under such disturbing conditions? Brave you are, if you can.

73

What after all do you want? You are not clear. Fogs all around. Your peace is challenged. Your sadhana is challenged. You are meeting defeat after defeat. You wish no opposition and yet like to be called a hero. Hurrah, did I teach you all this so far? You have failed very badly in the first paper of 'Mental Equilibrium'.

Shanti! Calm! Poise!

Unruffled quiet. Enter inside. Repeat his name. You are a brave child. Utilize the present defeat in perfecting your mental base.

To err is human. It is willed by divine force. It yields a fine reward if only you do not repeat the old mistakes. Can you imagine a lotus without mud, a pearl without the oyster? From mistakes comes immense purity.

Guru Poornima! Revive the zeal. Refresh the mind. Dedicate anew. Resolve tangibly. Test your sincerity, love and purity; offer your restlessness, unquiet, etc. to me.

Neemgaon (Maharashtra), July 13, 1960

The 16th is your birthday! Be in tune! The 16th is the day of constant and ceaseless sumiran. The 16th is the day of the birth of a new vigour and zeal for sadhana. The 16th – a reminder, an accelerator and yet a fresh push. The 16th – calm and peaceful!

Nothing is stationary in life. Disturbances as well as dissatisfaction are mental reactions. They pass away even as winter clouds. They flow like a stream into a river. They are lost in the past.

Real life is beyond the limits of the mind. Everlasting ananda is far beyond the mind. Mind is the seat of various pleasant and unpleasant feelings. Mind is the womb of sukha and dukha. Mental balance is a sadhana; it is a means to another end. Even as japa is a means to pratyahara for good dharana, likewise mental balance also is an essential item of sadhana in pratyahara. Equilibrium is different from

74

endurance. It is a quality of understanding the futility and perishability of every type of event. Equilibrium is that quality when your *self* has become a witness of all events. So long as you consider yourself a doer, you must enjoy as well as suffer the consequences.

Life is a sarai. Relatives are but travellers. Nobody can help you spiritually. If you do not empty your mind of all thoughts, you will not attain his grace. Various thoughts are obstacles. Thoughts regarding work alone are not obstacles. Daydreaming will delay the yogic process. Recollection of joy, etc., will draw you back.

On the eve of the 16th, I wish you a successful meditation.

Neemgaon, September 1, 1960

That voice which you heard during concentration was a faint expression of your inner voice. That will get clearer as and when you make progress.

Yes, your motor is now in speed. Fear not. You *have* to realize. Nothing can harm you even a bit. Charge your mind with faith and confidence. Please be aware of *that* power which is evolving in you day by day and which has begun to work through you. Now most things are being done by that power.

So, you are becoming free from the notion of doership.

At any cost, maintain perpetual equilibrium in life.

The force which was sleeping in you is waking up. It is gradually possessing your being. Ultimately it will possess you in full to the extent that you will not even remember yourself. Guru is always blessing you. He is eager to see you enlightened. I am glad that you have so intelligently followed the preliminaries and higher courses of yoga. What remains now is realization.

Mental as well as physical purity are essential. Become thick-skinned. Continue mental japa all throughout. Constant and ceaseless awareness is the way. Mind is to be rendered free and immune from all shocks. Ever calm, happy and cheerful! Every leisure is to be utilized for a flight in the spiritual land. Every minute is precious for a yogi. Every second is precious for a real sadhu. Time is fleeting; therefore, let us stop unyogic thinking. Maintain yogic introversion all throughout. No holiday from sadhana; no reserved hours for sadhana; regular, constant, unceasing and in various ways. No reflection on the past. No anticipation of the future. Always in the present, immediate present.

Plug your ears smoothly with clean cotton during nada yoga abhyasa. This is for the night-time practice. This provision will avoid shoulder strain. Japa and pranayama together in equal proportion along with plugging the ears will help you. You can do that in the morning also if you like and need to.

Keep unceasing engagement please. Have unbreakable peace and tender devotion. Be deaf to the world. Kill curiosity. Strength, beauty and peace! Feel it within thee.

Never sleep as others do. Lie down and meditate. Let sleep come through meditation. Beware that your thoughts don't loaf and roam aimlessly when you lie down to sleep.

Letters to Satyabrat

What is God?

If I swear now that I would not utter his name, somehow, to my utmost surprise, his name would come to my lips.

Once a newly born child was brought up in a jungle, away from society, under the care of a trained nurse, so that he may not be told or taught anything about God. At the age of eighteen he asked the nurse, "Who made the sun?"

He was sent into seclusion so that he wouldn't think of God. They wanted to see if the thought of God was inherent in man or was it a concept which was inherited from parents and society? But they found that the child felt there must be *someone* who created the sun.

We see around us a great universe. There must be someone who created that. Beyond these forms there must be someone immortal. This is how the common man inferred God.

A few men grew impatient to *know* that 'reality'. They renounced the world, led a life of great introversion and rigorous austerities; until at last they came to know of that light of lights. We call them seers. Aspirants seeking truth gathered round such seers, who imparted wisdom unto their disciples.

We first went to such seers and bowed unto them in all reverence, because they were the torch lights of knowledge. With their grace alone we came to know something about our master.

In our childhood we felt that there was nothing greater than our toys. When we grew a little more in age, we felt that there was nothing as significant as our dresses and society. Gradually, we came in contact with saints. Their divinity influenced our minds. We felt thus: even as air cannot be seen, various emotions cannot be apprehended, subtle vibrations cannot be perceived, likewise there is *something*, which too cannot be seen.

You might argue: the thing which exists must be seen. If God exists, we must be able to see him. Let me tell you, how

79

can you see everything of the world? There are certain things which you can't either see or explain, but you can feel them.

For instance, you cannot see fragrance, but you feel it. An ant bites you; you cannot see the pain, but you can feel it. Even a blind person can feel it. Even if you do not have ears or eyes, you will definitely know the taste of a rasagulla.

Through the eyes we see. Through the ears we hear. Through the tongue we taste; through the nose we smell; through the skin we feel touch. God is beyond the reach of these five senses. You cannot touch him with the physical hands. You cannot see him with the physical eyes.

If we cannot see a thing with our eyes, it does not exist, it is all false – this is how you are arguing at this moment.

May I ask you how many thoughts are coming to your mind at this moment? Are you able to see them? If not, do you dare to deny their existence?

Just as you cannot see thoughts, can't see the air, the butter in milk, a seed in the soil, a tree in the seed, a hen in an egg, or a child in the womb, likewise there is *something* which you can't see and which is beyond the reach of the five senses and the mind.

In order to see a distant object, you must take the help of binoculars. Through binoculars alone you can see two persons standing at a distance. You do not have binoculars, so you say you can't see anyone. You must either believe me because I have binoculars; or else you will have to see them yourself by procuring binoculars.

If you do not have the inner vision or sukshma drishti, go to the saints, who know the way.

Scientists say that there are mountains and ancient sea beds on the moon. Can you see them? Either you must have a powerful lens to see all that by yourself, or else you must have faith in those who proclaim the truth. Not everybody possesses so much inner wisdom; therefore, one has to rely upon the seers.

Right you are. There can be a few fools in this world; but how can the majority be foolish? If a few self-styled and frustrated intellectual giants deny the existence of God, I feel I would only land myself in logical errors by accepting their faith. It is not that I condemn the atheists; but I have somehow come to feel that they are erring and erring terribly in broad daylight by denying something which they have never cared to search for and seek out.

So never entertain such thoughts in your mind as are hovering at present. Never say that you will not worship him and do sadhana just because you do not see him. So long as you do not believe in him, you will not realize him.

In order to solve an algebraic sum, you have to say: 'supposing $3X$ plus Y is equal to 3'. If the student argues with his teacher as how '$3X$ plus Y is equal to 3', the teacher would only tell him to stop arguing and would insist upon supposing it in order to get a correct answer.

If while merely solving a sum we have to have faith in the supposed formulas, why talk of it when we are solving this greatest problem involving God and his creation?

Rishikesh, January 13, 1956

You will have to awaken love for God. You may even meditate for the whole lifetime without achieving any tangible result. The reason is simple: you do not have love for God. What is the use of meditating on a zero or a flower when the mind oscillates? You cherish love for mundane things, yet you complain about failure in sadhana.

What is love? *Constant remembrance and awareness of the beloved Lord and a keen longing to unite with him.* If there is no love in you, rest assured that you won't have his darshan. There is no fun in your going to Badrinath, if you fail to love God. Renunciation is a joke, sannyasa a mockery, if the aspirant lacks in bhakti. No man who lacks love for God will ever realize the divine glory.

You can get everything in the world except bhava and love for him. You can awaken that love from within yourself.

81

It is already there. It is trying to find an expression. Pray unto him to bless you with bhakti.

Prayers should emerge from the bottom of your heart. Prayers must come out in the form of perfect self-expression. Prayers that are true and original are at once heard and accepted by the Lord. Borrowed prayers are not original. Classical prayers are not true. True and original prayer is that prayer which represents your inner condition and is expressed in the language you understand well.

Prayer can't be taught in a school or a convent. I say prayer need not be taught at all. Every man has in him the virtue of praying, which can be manifested by means of bhakti. What one needs to know is that in him there lies a divine force which, if awakened, can render anything possible. Beware of artificial, ambiguous, borrowed and mechanical prayers; they will have to be kept off the list.

Prayers you have often heard in ashrams, temples and in mass congregations can be anything but 'prayers'. They are surface superimpositions which, when needed, dwindle into airy nothings. Such prayers belong to the department of intellect, while I wish to awaken that prayer which is an expression of your inner bhava and feelings.

Regarding meditation. I will initiate you into the yoga of meditation gradually. You should not be in a hurry. However, you have to bear in mind that dhyana yoga is the key. It does not mean that you have to put yourself under undue strain from now until then. At present sumiran alone will do. Sumiran yoga will by itself culminate in dhyana when the proper time comes.

Again, I don't prefer direct meditation. Dhyana is the seventh step of raja yoga. What about the preparatory sadhanas? Without practising preparatory sadhanas such as japa, asanas, pranayamas, dharana, nama japa, nama sankirtan, sattwic diet, celibacy, self-improvement, mental balance, etc., you mean to say I should initiate you into esoteric meditation? Don't be in a hurry. Be patient and persevering, sincere and earnest.

82

Meditation should come upon the aspirant without any personal effort. It is only then that it will culminate in samadhi. Please bear in mind that if the meditation is not spontaneous, as other thoughts are, its fruits will not be abiding.

Rishikesh, January 28, 1956

You have put a nice question, whether all saints can guide us or not, before they have direct intuitive knowledge.

If you have not seen Kedarnath, first hear from one who has seen it. You come to me and ask whether I have seen Kedarnath. It may be that I have not seen the place. However, when I say something about Kedarnath, there is no doubt that Kedarnath is somewhere in the world. This is the first truth. You asked me about Kedarnath and I told you that I had not seen the place. You went to someone else who said that he had seen Kedarnath.

Thus there are two types of saints. The first type is called brahmashrotriya, the other brahmanishtha.

He who has heard from guru and learnt from Vedic scriptures about God is a brahmashrotriya. We should believe him as well because he knows about the great being. He who has realized God and has direct intuitive experience is called a brahmanishtha.

Thus you can acquire knowledge about Him from every holy man. This is the first step towards yoga or communion.

Rishikesh, February 15, 1956

In order to have direct knowledge of God you must plunge into yoga sadhana. It is only then that you will realize him as the creator as well as the 'soul and stuff' of the creation.

God is not separate from creation. He has expressed himself in these creations. Even as from gold many

83

ornaments are made, the ornaments being nothing but gold in fact; even as from mud various pots are fashioned, those being nothing but mud in fact; likewise the creation is but his manifestation. It is not different from him. Everything here is an expression of consciousness absolute.

Ornaments without gold are nowhere. Pots without mud are nowhere. Similarly, creation is nowhere without him.

Call him 'Rama'. Rama means the one who is immanent in all. He is sakara as well as nirakara, saguna, as well as nirguna, vyakta as well as avyakta. You can meditate either upon his form or formlessness.

Nirakara and sakara are one and the same. Whenever you meditate on your Ishta and merge yourself in him, you forget yourself. Gradually the two become one, and thus you get the non-dual consciousness or adwaita anubhuti.

If you consider God as all pervading, you can see him in any form. Thus there is no harm if you consider guru as God. First of all be aware that he is all pervading.

The other truth you should know is that God is omniscient, i.e. all-knowing. It means that God knows everything about time, space and object.

The third truth you should know is that he is omnipotent. It means that he can do everything.

Rishikesh, March 4, 1956

Why this confusion regarding sakara and nirakara upasana? Did not I tell you that both are his attributes?

If you are not clear whether you should do nirakara upasana or sakara upasana, you will not reach anywhere. You can realize him by either of the two ways. These modes of meditation are not different at all. When your mind is merged in sakara, nirakara dawns automatically. Whenever you meditate on the photo of Rama, you get his sakara anubhava. This is the first stage. Nirakara is the culmination of sakara, while sakara is acceptance of nirakara.

The mind spontaneously and rapidly gets merged in a form. So a bhakta meditates on the form of Rama or Krishna or Shiva or Guru. God reveals himself in and through that very form. This is nothing but his grace that he, being nirakara, comes into the sphere of the mind for his devotees.

So long as the mind does not merge in him, and so long as it does not forget its individual consciousness, God cannot be realized. The mind should lose its identity in God-consciousness. It is then that he appears.

Therefore, you should unhesitatingly choose one of the modes of sadhana for consuming the individual consciousness.

Rishikesh, March 7, 1956

Asato maa sat gamaya!
Lead me from unreal to real!

Do you understand the secret of your lukewarm love for your Ishta Devata? You haven't developed as much attachment for him as you have for wife and wealth. There is no use accusing dharma sadhana, guru mantra and God if you have failed to develop intense longing to unite with him.

Why does your mind swing like a pendulum? It is not the mind which is to be blamed. It is you and only you who have been doing sadhana without bhava and feeling. Did you ever try to channel your dissipated emotions towards he who can consume them in toto? You need a whip now.

You know that lady who has been living on fruits and milk for the last twenty-five years. Where does she stand now? There itself where she started her journey twenty-five years ago. She still remains a slave of anger, greed, back-biting, crooked-mindedness, egoism and passion. Do you dare to say that she has derived any perceptible benefit by remaining on fruits and milk for twenty-five years? No, no,

Satyabrat, this is *not* the way. Please don't get into this rut and religion of old ladies.

So long as your mind doesn't rest in the centre and so long as it is not overwhelmingly emotional after him, no amount of fasting, pilgrimage, shastra adhyayan and puja path will confer divine experience.

I advised that lady when she approached me for his darshan in quite a different way. I instructed her: *detach* and *attach* (vairagya and abhyasa). It means this. Supposing a water stream is flowing. You want to irrigate your land with its water. You will have to channel the water towards your fields to be irrigated. So first you detach the stream from its original course; next step you attach it to your fields by means of a canal.

In the same way you have to withdraw your attachment from mundane affairs, which is the process of vairagya, and then merge the same in God-consciousness, which is abhyasa. The mind, which is naturally inclined towards petty objects and pleasures, should be brought back every time it loses touch with the centre. The thoughts which naturally follow the twin trends of attraction and repulsion – raga and dwesha – will have to be turned therefrom and be led towards the seat of the supreme through the royal road of anasakti.

Bhakti is a divine gift; it is given by him. Unfortunately we have misappropriated the divine wealth in satisfying our worldly whims and fancies, passions and fashions. The gift of God – which love is – has been consumed by wife, children, property, kith, kin, name and fame. Thus man has lost the capital together with the interest. What remains with him now, is a bundle of reserve bank notes; and that, by force of circumstances, he offers to the Lord at Kedarnath as 'puja'. Now let him withdraw the love from mundane objects and direct the same towards the supreme Lord.

So you have understood what I mean when I say 'detach and attach'.

No use fasting if your mind is fast running after evil-mindedness. What is the harm if you eat and drink well and

86

lead an inner life of purity and peace? A non-vegetarian friend with altruism in his head and hands and sacrifice in his every nerve is by all means better than that vegetarian and self-styled pundit who is engrossed in black marketing, adulteration, exploitation and anti-social activities. Therefore, it is better to be a simple man with noble virtues than to be a nobleman with ignoble vices. Then what? Be a man of God, friend of all, brother of all believers and master of your own self!

Tamaso maa jyotir gamaya!
Lead me from darkness to light!

The moment I was closing this letter, the Lord's upadesha flashed into my mind at once, wherein he sums up the teachings of the Gita before his beloved disciple, Arjuna. These are the lines:

"Having renounced all notions of avidya, come unto me alone for shelter; I shall make you free from all sins thereof; ye worry not."

Please note 'come unto me alone for shelter'. Here the Lord asks us to lay all the burdens at his feet. Yes, he means total surrender where we not only yield to the pressure of circumstances, but also voluntarily go to him with hands folded, head bent, ego surrendered and heart divinized.

So long as the wife does not submit herself to the husband in her entirety, she cannot be close to him to the extent she expects to be. When she submits herself entirely, she undoubtedly gets complete rights over him and all that belongs to him. The secret of this 'gain' is hidden in 'totally giving' the things of fleeting values against the 'thing' of absolute value. Yes, you give yourself; and you not only gain him, you regain yourself also.

The sea tells the river, "Oh darling! If you want to become one with me, you will have to merge yourself in me and lose your individuality." In the same way, if you want to gain him, you will have to take back all the attention you have given to the world and offer the same unto your beloved. No

87

sooner do you offer your attention unto him than the yoga of meditation manifests in full.

Give the gold to the devil, but spare love and attention for God. He is not in need of your gold, plantains or sweets. He is feeding infinite universes from *that* time. The only offering to be made unto him is your attention and love. Unless you turn the gaze from the fleeting shadows and fading beauties, you cannot expect redemption from sin and misery. Unless you turn the gaze from worldly pleasures and skin-deep lust, how can you be happy and peaceful? How can you gain the best by slaying your own soul?

You are a traveller sitting on a train bound for Delhi. Many stations will come on your way, no doubt; but you should not get down at any of these stations. Remember that you are destined for Delhi, and nowhere else. The duties you render to your wife and children cannot be your ultimate destiny. However, you *have* to travel through these wayside stations in order to reach your destination. You have to discharge your duties side by side with your spiritual sadhana. Should you consider those stations your ultimate goal, you will be left alone on the platform quite shelterless and ignored. Pravritti marga is the path which leads the jiva to its ultimate destination. Nivritti is an attitude of being ever aware of the goal, which is moksha. Ye, walk upon the path of life with perfect awareness of your spiritual destiny!

Work you must; for there is no other way. One has to work to live and support the family. This is the first step on the staircase. As soon as the foot reaches the next step, let one take the first foot off the last step and place it on the next one.

So the way is love and surrender. Now you can meditate on him. This is bhakti yoga. Bhakti yoga is the way of communion through love and surrender.

Let one call him as lovingly as a wife would call her husband or her only son.

Let one remember him as a lady would remember her precious golden necklace presented by her husband on their wedding night, and which was stolen a few minutes back.

Let one have such desire for him in his heart as a lady would have for showing her friends the fine nylon saris sent by her husband from foreign places.

Neither in temples, nor by ringing bells and blowing conches, nor even by waving the arati and clapping the hands does one see him; but verily it is love, a dynamic and creative type of love one holds and nourishes in one's heart, by which one sees him within as well as without.

Mrityor maa amritam gamaya!
Lead me from death to immortality!

Yet another step towards surrender! And I believe most of your doubts will be cleared.

Why should you bother about the house repairs when the landlord is already there to do it for you? This is his temple; let him do as he likes. Surrender will have to be backed by this attitude.

In the same way you should always bear in mind that not only this body but your wife and relatives and property also are his gifts. Not for a moment should you forget this fact that he alone looks after all your needs. This attitude will not only remove worries and fears, but it will also bestow immense spiritual stamina.

Why do we suffer from insomnia, headache, blood pressure and other similar diseases? Don't you think it's because we lack the necessary quality of perfect self-surrender? I believe that there is something which by following we can remain at ease mentally as well as physically. You might call it anasakti; I call it atma samarpan or self-surrender. Anyway, both are the same.

The art of surrender is a virtue in itself. It must be complete. It must be one hundred percent. Half-hearted surrender is no surrender. Verbal surrender is no surrender. Surrender born of love is abiding and real.

Individual consciousness cannot be consumed by either of the two modes of sadhana if one lacks divine love for one's Ishtam. Therefore, you should first of all develop love for him. Divine love is realized through the grace of God and the blessings of saints. You can develop it through sakama bhakti also.

Those who practise nishkama bhakti do not have so much intense love. They are so dull and emotionless.

Sakama bhakti is not inferior to nishkama bhakti. It develops love for God. When your desires are fulfilled, your love for him is intensified. In the course of time, you will give up sakama bhakti of your own accord and start loving him for the sake of love.

Those who meditate upon him for the sake of realizing some desired end become merged in him sooner than those who meditate on him for nothing. Those who consider nishkama bhakti as superior to sakama bhakti do not know the truth in essence. You can get moksha even by practising sakama upasana. You can get nirvikalpa samadhi as well through sakama bhakti. It is a matter of one's experience and knowledge. You should totally give up the belief that if you meditate on him with sakama bhavana, you will not get moksha. There is no necessity for you to change the course of your bhavana and sadhana. At the point of merger sakama culminates into nirakara.

Please go on with your sakama upasana without hesitation. In due course it will surely consume the individual consciousness and culminate in nirakara.

Do you wonder as to how sakara is consumed by nirakara?

Still I don't blame you for this doubt. Sectarian preachers have caused a great confusion with regard to this point.

I personally know that meditation on a concrete object leads one to nirvikalpa samadhi. It is like this.

We can give any, or a particular, pattern to our mind. We can shape it either in the pattern of a woman, or a man, or a pot, or a watch, or a boy. When we meditate on Krishna, our mind assumes the form of Krishna, which gradually becomes consumed in self-consciousness, resulting in nirvikalpa samadhi.

When the mind merges in the form of the Ishta Devata, the sense consciousness is withdrawn. Unified consciousness of mind is awake. This too perishes when astral and causal awareness are merged in the 'thing-in-itself'.

Selection of the form of meditation must, therefore, be based on love. That is to say, you should select that object for meditation which would at once magnetize your mind and compel it to withdraw itself from all other objects.

Perfect introversion is only really possible when the mind has a better object to dwell upon. A better object is that one which the mind can comprehend with interest and intensity. Scattered extrovert tendencies of the mind can be easily collected and united around an impressive form. Mind loses its grip over objective consciousness when the object of meditation is lovely, interesting, attractive and fitting into the individual psychology.

Meditation on a *form* is nothing but nirakara upasana. When you meditate on Rama, it is meditation on your own soul, which is nirakara. The sakara is left outside. What you have in you now is a mental form. Your soul alone manifests itself *through* that form. Thus sakara upasana is but a form of atma upasana.

You can meditate on sakara, say a stone. That is meditation on atma. *Truth is within you.* Outer form is a basis for mystic flights in unknown lands. So go on meditating on one form until the mind merges in the wake of higher consciousness. You will know the truth yourself. If nothing appeals to you, select *Om* as a basis for dharana.

91

He has given you such a capable body and mind. Man is the most beautiful and privileged creation of God. If he felt that man needed some more beauty, he would have given him that too. But it appears that he was satisfied with man's mental perfection and psychic capacities.

The aim of your life is self-realization. It is better to be born as a dog or as a monkey than that man who leaves the world without realizing the self. What is the difference between such a man and an animal? You will have to be sincere. You will have to give up hypocrisy. You go to temples and take his name twice a day and you feel as if you have discharged your duty towards God, while it takes you the whole day to discharge the duties towards your family and society. What a pity!

Pain and pleasure may come on your way. The clouds of calamities may eclipse your inner shrine. But with nothing should you barter the peace of your soul. He alone who considers pain and pleasure as passing clouds and is always aware of his goal will be really happy.

You should have intense lagan for realization. Keep your goal before you. It is not compulsory to sit at one place and take his name. On the other hand, your whole life must be dedicated to his awareness. Every act of yours must become his worship. Whenever you get time, merge yourself in his sumiran, introvert your tendencies, peep within and experience joy.

Whenever you are free from occupations, try to feel that your body is becoming lighter and that you are experiencing pleasantness, thrills and serenity within you. You surely can't get such thrills from any worldly objects. Real life is a life of service, bhakti and yoga. Our eternal abode is the seat of Brahman. We all are pilgrims here.

God is in everything. He is in guru, in a stone, in Rama, Krishna, as well as in all. You can worship him in any form you like. I have allowed you to worship him in any manner possible. When the mind is merged in one rupa the light in us manifests itself.

Here is the difference between yourself and a saint. Certainly a saint has not descended from heaven; but he has unlocked the great *secret* and opened the knot through meditation. He has been able to peep inside and become one with God.

Delhi, June 21, 1956

Get up at four in the morning. Take a cup of tea if you feel drowsy. Do pranayama for a while without retention. While you inhale, feel that purity, love, fearlessness, vairagya, etc. are entering into you. While you exhale, feel that jealousy, hatred, impurity and fear are going out of you. Sit straight with full attention; don't take the support of the wall. Sit in padmasana, if you can. Chant a few kirtans loudly at first. Then repeat your mantra in beads. Japa mala arrests the extrovert consciousness. It locks the mind.

Don't postpone this item for old age. There is no guarantee that you will live for one hundred years. What if there is a war in 1964? There is no surety of one's life. You cross the road, a motor-truck runs you over; you talk to your friend, the next moment you are down with a heart attack. I advise you, therefore, to take up spiritual sadhana now.

Merge your mind in him through japa and dhyana. Bring his divine form on your mental plane. Pray unto him in all love. Open your heart unto him. Don't lock it with a big Godrej lock. Love is the key which will help you to open the lock. It will open the door of the cage, in which is enshrined the *golden bird*. The pathway towards it is sadhana. The strength to reach the cage is love. The key which opens the lock is concentration.

93

If you suffer from constipation, you will have headache, fever and all sorts of diseases. In the same way if you suffer from mental constipation, you will be unable to sleep. You will feel restless, dull and depressed. You will be worried and shocked.

How do you cure physical constipation? By taking Purgolax or fruit-salts. Thereby the constipated matter is thrown out of your body. Now you have no fever or any other physical complaint. You feel all right, very light and healthy. In the same way whenever you suffer from mental constipation, give a purgative to your mind. Prayer is the purgative which removes the fermented filth out of the system. It means that you should not hide anything from him. Speak everything unto him. Yes, go to him all naked and all empty. Though our beloved Lord knows everything, still we have to tell him in order to empty our minds of the filth. Place before him all your defects and actions. If you hide your emotions and desires from him, you will have to go to a chemist in order to purchase Saridone or Anacin.

Prayer is the most effective medicine, which won't cost you anything. Feel as if he is standing before you; you at his feet, kneeling down and saying unto him all your troubles, karmas, accomplishments, emotions and worries. Let it take one, two or three hours even. You will see that a lot of the mental burden has been taken off your shoulders.

Great difficulties confuse us. Clouds surround all over. Criticisms create restlessness. But with all that, if we sincerely take his name, adversities will pass away like winter clouds. We will be able to maintain a high rate of stamina and a balanced mind. We will not be puffed up by prosperity, nor shall we be disappointed by forced austerities. Take this divine anaesthesia.

Do nama sankirtan along with your family members in the evening. No pomp and show. Just sit together and sing his glories. There definitely is a great power inherent in his name. Do experience it.

A home where there is mutual peace, where husband and wife do not quarrel, where bitter taunts and harsh words are totally prohibited, where husband and wife respect each other at every step of life, where every family member knows how to 'forget and forgive', where every affair is treated in a spiritual light, verily that home is really a heaven on earth, a lovely divine garden laden with beautiful flowers of eternal fragrance.

Bring peace in your home. Keep the garden of family ever green and fragrant. Reorganize the scattered patterns of your home. Rebuild your house on the strong foundation of love, peace, unity and strength. Let every one of you have a different flute, but let the tunes of all be the same. If everybody starts playing different tunes, there will be a mess. Both of you should have one aim in life and help each other for its fulfilment. Try to understand each other. Never exchange harsh words. No bullet can really kill a man as the tongue does.

God is all-merciful. He forgives us any number of times. Even a thief can become a saint provided he makes a thorough changeover in his life. A public woman also can reach him provided she surrenders her entire being at his feet. Such instances are too many to be quoted here.

Never take into account the past history of a saint. See what does he tell you. It is very difficult to understand them. We mortals have a very bad habit of finding fault with others. We make the first mistake and ignore the important thing.

We can change our lives by changing the mode of our thinking. As you think, so you become. Whatever you are today is what you thought yesterday; and what you will be tomorrow is what you think today. Surely a man becomes great not by anything but by his karma and swabhava.

Religion, spiritual life, the philosophy of sadhana have nothing to do with the life hereafter. These things are meant for this life, to better this stage, to decorate this platform. If religion cannot solve the problem of this life, reject it. If spiritual life cannot afford to bestow peace on the soul of this body, dash it off. And, if sadhana cannot enrich your present existence with beauty and health, success and gold, kick it off. We do not want these things at all, if they are only for parloka. I love this life. I care to make this existence better. I wish to make this body hale and hearty, this mind quiet and peaceful. I love men more than they love stone gods. The more I mix with people, the more I have begun to love them. Love is a greater force than the law of religion. If water cannot cool your body, or food appease your hunger, love can do that.

Thus the children must be given the message '*be up and doing*'. Not even a single moment should they waste in useless pursuits. They must become adventurous and enterprising. How long can they depend on someone? Let them strengthen their willpower, decide something finally and plunge into it day and night. Success knows no rest. Life needs no procrastination. Death is a challenge, a warning, a call to get ready to face the realities of life, which are so thrilling, so romantic and so new.

Truth for today: in you there is that phase of consciousness which is to be discovered. That consciousness is a part of cosmic consciousness. It is the source and store of all knowledge, power and wisdom. That consciousness is gained by faith and practice.

Wisdom is just the manifestation of your own self in deep samadhi. Ishwara is just the manifestation of your inner consciousness.

Keep on supplying *this* oil to *that* lamp wherein is burning *this* light in all its glory and infancy. Let the light enlighten your soul.

There is none who denies the supreme creator of universes. Scientists too believe in a conscious and sentient cause. But belief itself will not better the scheme of life, will not divinize the life which is beset with baser elements.

The mere fact that we aim at bettering our earthly career is sufficient evidence that we live with God; not merely believe that *he is*. Faith in God is not a belief; it is a system of practising the ideals. What is the good of my persistent declarations about the existence of God if my life doesn't express it.

I think that the best method to work with both believers and non-believers is to be honest and spiritually silent. But this silence should not be interpreted as something which denies God. Satyam's affirmative noddings to both may be understood as frank admittance of the inability of the finite mind to deny or accept non-empirical truth. Rather, my 'yes' to both signifies the indescribability of his status, experience and reality. Please remember that 'yes' about God, as also 'no' about him, are neither contradictory, nor even two antagonistic attitudes. Both 'yes' and 'no' are two different attributes of him whom they visualize either positively or negatively.

Hence this philosophical compromise should unite different faiths, so that all may conjointly understand Satyam; of course, without losing their own stuff of faith. Well, we have to disagree with the views of hedonists, epicureans and animalistically demoralized individuals.

The best way to bring them round is regular training in yoga asanas. Of late, Satyam has come to realize this. Many careless individuals have taken to spiritual life just because they come to me to learn yoga asanas. Even those who hated spiritual life, but suffered physically, come to me and still come to get themselves yogically trained. You know what I do with them? I regulate their life itself. You see, I am bent upon reaching a 'way of life' – dharma I mean.

Those who are suffering may come to me. Those who wish to know him may come to me. Those who love me may come to me. Those who deny God may come to me. Let them surround me in any manner they like. I will give them a 'way of life' which will be practical, divine and trouble-free. And thus we end the logical discussion about God's existence and absence; for both are his attributes – and attributes are inseparably integrated with the object proper. Satyam is not wavering. He is only adamant in frankly accepting the conclusion of the Upanishads.

> *The sun does not shine there, nor do the moon and stars.*
> *From where the speech returns along with the mind,*
> *not having found him.*
> *Not this, not this.*

No honest man has ever boasted that he saw God, although we infer that a few such souls would have had twinkling and lightning glimpses of the reality somehow. Hence, let us not be speculative and visionary. On the other hand, we must be immediately practical, careful, divine and honest.

Jamshedpur, April 12, 1957

Bodily ailments are great obstacles in the spiritual path. The common and main disease from which the majority of the world's population is suffering is constipation, which is the root cause of all sorts of dangerous diseases. Amongst other obstacles, stomach trouble really hampers the progress of the aspirant towards God-realization. In advanced age this gives all the more trouble if proper care is not taken. Besides a regulated and light diet, I suggest for you a few yoga asanas; and if you perform them regularly for at least half an hour daily, I am sure you will enjoy good health and long life, peace and prosperity.

I had thrown some light on yogic asanas in one of my letters. Now I suggest a few pranayama exercises. If you practise them regularly and systematically, not only will you have better health but it would also help you in concentration and meditation. Pranayama goes hand in hand with yogasanas. By regular practice you can maintain a higher standard of health, vigour and vitality. Its practice regulates the action of the heart, lungs and brain. It promotes digestion and circulation of the blood. Combined with yogasanas, these remove all sorts of diseases and bestow most wonderful health on the practitioner.

Breathing plays a very important part in maintaining the body in sound condition. These days our friends do not realize its importance. Hence their bodies decay early, their breathing being irregular. If one controls the breath, the mind is also controlled. If the mind and the prana are both kept under control, one gets liberation from birth and death and attains immortality. There is an intimate connection between the mind, prana and the senses. In short, pranayama is the control of the vital forces of the body. It is regulation of the breath to have perfect control of the life current.

The first stage is to master the pranas and the next is pranayama. You need not wait till you have mastery over asanas before practising pranayama. That pose is best which can be kept for a long time comfortably. Practise asanas, and side by side you can practise pranayama.

You will have good appetite, cheerfulness, strength, courage, vigour, vitality and good concentration of mind. There should be no strain in pranayama. Whenever you feel uneasy and depressed, you may practise pranayama. Inhale and exhale very slowly without making any sound. The practice of retention produces heat, as well as increasing the span of life. The mind becomes one-pointed after the practice of pranayama. The body becomes strong and healthy, free from all diseases.

99

Mouna should be observed during the practice. Take a light diet; observe brahmacharya.

Pranayama may be practised in a dry and well-ventilated place, twice a day, morning and evening, on an empty stomach. Do not bathe immediately after asanas and pranayama. Wait for at least half an hour. Do not wipe the perspiration with a towel; rub it in with your hands. Do not expose your perspiring body to chill and cold air. Be regular in the practice. Take sattwic food.

In the beginning, you might feel peculiar sensations about which you should not be unnecessarily alarmed and thereby give up the practice. I am sending you a book by separate post for further guidance and practice.

Raipur, August 1, 1957

In my previous letters I had suggested to you a few important yogasanas and easy pranayamas, which I am sure you will continue with sincerely. You will not only get rid of physical complications and enjoy sound health, but you will also experience a strange peace of mind. Every disorder in your nervous system, metabolism and respiratory system will vanish.

If, however, for some reason you cannot find enough time for yogasanas and pranayama on any day, you can practise a few rounds of surya namaskara. This is a dynamic form of worship of the sun, the source of cosmic energy.

Surya namaskara is best practised exactly at sunrise, with the body exposed to the sun's rays. Abundance of health-giving sunrays revive the cells and other systems of the body within a short period.

Regarding the method of doing surya namaskara, I am sending you a small booklet by separate post.

Preplanned divine arrangements and ordinances can't be written off. There is no escape for individual freedom. It is always better to dance with unseen tunes and feel happy under all changes and disposals.

Divine steps are mysterious. We, who are plunged in avidya, cannot make anything of his plans. To us, his plans seem to be whimsical and his orders beyond understanding.

A bhakta has full faith in him. He will accept his arrangements as a form of divine grace. The real devotee does not murmur, complain or grumble over the past.

If the soul is sat-chit-ananda, why should he be a victim of sorrow, misery, worry, conflicts and other forces? We repeat *'Shivoham'* which means, 'I am that ananda swarupa atma'. Why does this blissful soul experience sorrow and joy?

Such questions arise in the minds of many people who want to know the real implications of the soul and its nature. The answer in brief is as follows.

Just as a king, in a dream, sees himself as a beggar, while in reality he is a king, in the same way this soul imagines the feelings of sorrow and joy. This is what our scriptures say.

When this soul is all-joy and all-knowledge, why then this delusion? Why does it mistake itself for something else?

I sleep at night and dream that I am a grihastha, when, in fact, I am a sannyasi. I know the truth only when I wake up. So I was a sannyasi, and I am still a sannyasi; however, just for some time in the middle, I did not know that I was a sannyasi. Similarly, I am atma in fact, though I have *somehow* forgotten my real nature.

The question then arises as to why this soul is deluded. Why and when did this delusion cover the soul? Nobody can answer properly. All the Vedas and shastras are silent

101

about this question. We can simply say that the Lord himself is just playing a wonderful play.

If you insult me, I will definitely feel bad because my indriyas are receptive to it. Once I sleep, even if you insult me, I will not be affected by it. So this soul, when connected with maya, experiences sorrow and joy and becomes as it were a victim of the positive and negative charges of nature.

The electric bulb shines while the fan stands still, although both can be connected to the powerhouse through wires. Why? Because the bulb is plugged in and the fan stands disconnected. In the same way, when we plug ourselves into the world and its objects, we are affected by them and consequently we experience sorrow and joy.

Where is the root of sorrow? They consider sorrow to be anadi. But in my opinion, the root of sorrow is not far from us; it is in us. It is rooted in our minds and indriyas. If we control our mind by yoga, or surrender it unto his lotus feet, our miseries will come to an end.

Through the five jnanendriyas and five karmendriyas together with manas and buddhi, chitta and ahamkara and the pranas, we experience the past in the form of joy and sorrow. When the jivatma connects itself with these nineteen tattwas, it becomes the experiencer of all sorrow and joy.

This body is a kshetra and there is one kshetragya in it; Shiva, Rama, sat-chit-ananda, soul, call it by any name you will. When this kshetragya identifies itself with the kshetra and its essential factors, it experiences all that happens with the kshetra, i.e. within the body.

Take a fresh coconut; break the shell. The inner kernel also will be broken. Now take another dry coconut and break it. The shell will break, but the inner portion will remain unaffected. Why? Because the kernel has now detached itself from the shell. Even so, if we disidentify our soul from the body, we will not be affected by what happens to the body.

Take another example. Ramesh and Suresh are unknown to each other. Someone dies in Ramesh's family. Suresh will not be affected by that death because he has no connection

102

with Ramesh. Next year the daughter of Suresh is given in marriage to Ramesh. From now onwards Suresh will definitely be affected by every event occurring in Ramesh's family. Why? Because he has connected himself with them. In the same way the soul has identified itself with prakriti since time immemorial.

What then have we to do to disidentify the soul from prakriti? Just as we separate butter from milk, or rice from its chaff, in the same way we have to separate purusha and prakriti tattwas through sadhana. Even as we take out pig-iron and steel from the raw material with the help of a blast furnace, likewise we have to separate the real by removing the unreal matters with the help of yogic fire.

Just as we separate gold from the gold-stone by setting aside the non-gold elements, in the same way we have to detach and discover the soul which is lying dormant in the folds of prakriti. The method is sadhana.

Supposing you go to a jungle. There a lion passes in front of you and goes away without inflicting any harm on you. All this is over, no doubt; but what will be the state of your mind? Full of fear, intense fear! You will continue to see the imaginary lion before you. His teeth and terrible face will come before your mind as real as anything. This is the laya stage of chitta.

The husband of a young lady died. Even then she used to feel as if he were with her and she used to feed him. Her sons said that she herself ate the food for two persons. Of course, she has come to know the right state of affairs now.

This is an example of the tanmaya stage of mind, when the mind has merged in one. Until we do not merge our mind, prakriti and purusha will not be separated. The swan is well known for separating water from milk. This bird is said to be white and aquarian. Its dearest abode is mansarovar or the mind-lake which is situated in the vicinity of Kailash. I have seen the bird. I have known it in full. I not only know hamsa, I know param hamsa also, who is the master of the art of separating milk from water, or consciousness from matter.

103

When you go to the burning ghat at the dead of night, you feel as if there are people all around, as if there are many sounds coming from a distance, and as if some ghost has come. At this fearful juncture the state of mind is possessed by an intense belief and fear and because of this you see a figure as clearly as anything.

In the *Ishavasya Upanishad*, we read that the face of truth is covered with a golden cover. Yes, this all-blissful soul is as if covered by three curtains. We have to tear off these veils. There are three veils and seven doors. Beyond these three and those seven is the field of atma or purusha where there is infinite light and bliss. As long as we do not know these three veils, those seven gates and that inner purusha, and as long as we do not realize that there is a great power in us, we cannot get rid of sorrow and miseries.

This soul is nirakara *in essence*. Its name is Shiva, Rama, atma, etc. This soul lives within the folds of prakriti. Around this soul there is an extension of consciousness up to many crores of miles, where Narayana sleeps. One who has entered into satya loka by dint of sadhana and has raised his soul high in the sky, knows and sees Lord Vishnu in ksheer sagar. He sleeps in the limitless ocean.

What I want to tell you is that this body is not only as much as you see. Beyond the phases of perception and experience, we have seen in it an infinite power. Within the folds of the body there lies the power of homogeneous consciousness.

The consciousness is hidden beyond seven gates. You have to discover the soul in the eighth. Unlock the gates one by one. Lo, he is there. Soar high in the sky. Climb those staircases, which are seven in number. Beyond the seventh is a temple resplendent with lights, equivalent to infinite suns. There is a pure bird sitting over a thousand-petalled lotus – silent and sweet. And know it again through me that this temple is in you; and this bird is within that temple.

Our great Upanishad tells us that "the one who stays in me, who is my essence, but whom I don't know and who

104

governs me from inside, is the soul, the inner ruler and immortal". The soul is *in* this body and not *the* body.

How to realize this purusha? How to reach up to it? By controlling the mind. How to control the mind? There are various methods to control it. I will tell you the best and easiest method.

When a box of precious ornaments is lost, we become introverted. When there is some great problem confronting us, we do not even notice our surroundings. Many people pass by, but we see no one. This introverted condition is available to everybody who knows its technique. When a lady does some stitching work, she sings a lullaby to her baby; her hands automatically move; side by side she talks to her friend about her home and family. This shows that work can go on even if our mind is introverted.

In order to have one-pointed introversion you will have to know the method of concentration and meditation. Once you know the method, you can very easily practise it. Gradually the mind can be brought under control. Meditation perfects the process of splitting purusha from prakriti. It is like this.

When we perfect meditation on Rama's picture, we can see him before us as real as anything. The nirakara *becomes* sakara. The consciousness is separated from matter or prakriti. The mind doesn't exist at this moment. When you concentrate on him, you actually concentrate upon your atma, which reveals itself before you in your cherished form. It is your atma, which comes to you from beyond the seven gates. It is the *swan of the temple*, which is seen by you in the medium of the form you meditated upon.

When you are in samadhi, the seven gates are opened; the veils are rent asunder. That is the reason why I ask you to meditate. No sooner than the mind merges and the meditation is keen and progressive, the soul will begin to express itself. Lo, the light is seen clearly. That same soul, which makes your body and mind work, comes before you as sakara.

Bhakti is the simplest way to manifest the nirakara soul. This soul, the great power dormant in us, manifests through

105

sattwic, rajasic and tamasic forms. Sattwic materialization gives peace, bliss and moksha. Rajasic and tamasic materializations react upon a sadhaka and cause misery, pain and even death sometimes.

In my last letter I had dealt in great length with your questions about the real nature of the soul and the method to obtain permanent bliss through meditation. Now I am giving you some hints on the subject of concentration.

You know how to get permanent joy; but at the particular moment you forget everything. A blind man wanted to catch a running calf. He himself fell down. But once he regains his eyesight, he will definitely catch the calf sooner or later.

In order to retain and experience that joy you must have strength. Divine bliss and joy demand inner strength to bear it. You do not get that joy because you have not prepared your mind. So long as your indriyas wander in the objects, you will not get that bliss. So long as the gopis are engrossed in their family affairs, they will not hear the flute of Krishna. Simply saying that you are the blissful soul will not do. You might go in silence and think over it and believe that you are not this body but the soul; you are not the horse but the master. You might as well develop a little faith in it, but by merely saying that you are bliss absolute, you can't become that. You must possess the required qualifications. So when you assert that you are blissful soul etc., you must live up to your claims. You must realize it. You must experience it.

You know, the jiva has four phases of consciousness. The first phase of consciousness is sense consciousness, i.e. jagriti. The second is subjective consciousness, i.e. swapna. The third phase is dormant consciousness, i.e. sushupti. The fourth is turiya or superconsciousness. Beyond this is turiyateeta or transcendental consciousness. Yogis have witnessed these phases.

106

Experiences and motions of objective consciousness depend upon the senses and mental activities. Perceptions of subjective consciousness are reflective projections dependent upon objective experiences. They can be experienced within our own selves because of the subtlety of mental vision. You can even see the biggest objects within you in a very subtle form. Dormant impressions are projected and reflected upon in dreams. Dreams are manifestations of samskaras. Samskaras are born of experiences. Experiences are born of actions, karmas. Thus the numerous impressions of previous incarnations are also manifested in dreams. So we see hitherto unseen things also.

Subtler than dream consciousness is the sushupti stage. The individual consciousness becomes dormant and is temporarily suspended because of the inactive conditions of the senses and mind. However, it doesn't lose self-consciousness even at that stage. It becomes free from sense experiences just for some time. It contains in it the seeds of reincarnation. It maintains in it the usual link of individuality. There is no loss of the seeds of objective consciousness in this stage of jiva. There is every possibility for the revival of continuous individual consciousness.

Turiya is samadhi. It is that fire wherein all impressions dormant in an individual are burnt in toto. Not only total merger of mind and its vrittis, but total annihilation of every superimposition also takes place during samadhi or turiya. No possibility of remanifestation or reincarnation of individuality is allowed to exist. Veil after veil is rent asunder. Phase after phase of individual consciousness is transcended. The yogi soars high, taking mystic flights from bhu loka to bhuvar loka, then to swar loka, maha loka, jano loka and tapo loka, until he reaches satya loka – the land of reality.

The yogi gradually awakens his inner consciousness. He tears the first veil of sense consciousness and thus ascends to satya loka, which is in the soul. Satya loka is the aim of all yogas. It is reached through yogic concentration, meditation and samadhi. It is only here that the purusha stands separately in his divine glory and divine power. It is here that he exclaims, "I am bliss absolute; I am knowledge absolute; I am Shiva; I am all." It is here that he really abides in his own self. This is the supreme abode. This is the ultimate experience of all yogas. This is that stage where the consciousness is devoid of all dualities and erroneous notions.

So your bottle should be strong enough not to break when boiling water is poured into it. Let me tell you frankly that until you have concentrated your mind on one form of God by any method, you will not be able to realize the atman. This is a great truth.

God is within you. I can accept any challenge from non-believers. It is the light of your nirakara consciousness, which comes to you in sakara form. Saints and great men have shaken the world from time to time with this great power alone; for it is within everybody. The thing you want is already in you. It is outside also. But you will not get anything from outside. You will have to peep within in order to realize it. It is only then that it will be revealed unto you.

Whichever form you perceive in dhyana is just a sakara rupa of your nirakara atman. Beyond gross consciousness, there is astral consciousness. Beyond that even is causal consciousness or the karana sharira. When a man is awake, his powers are limited. When his sense capacities are withdrawn, the powers are proportionately increased. When he is emptied of all sense capacities, sense experiences and sense vibrations, his omnipotence, omniscience and omnipresence find unlimited scope of expression which hitherto was obstructed by impurity, distraction and illusion.

The above-mentioned threefold capacities are expressed in different degrees, depending upon the yogic achievements of a sadhaka. It is only when full-fledged yoga is achieved that he wields these three powers in full swing. These powers are achieved in different stages of yoga.

Inner voice is one of the expressions of these powers. It is something which is beyond all conceptions of empirical

108

knowledge. It is a compelling force from within. It does not require any basis for warning, suggesting and helping. It helps the sadhaka at every stage of life. It helps him to visualize future events beforehand. Inner voice is the voice of God, as it were, from the heavens.

So this soul in us is all-knowing and has the greatest powers within it. Saints have adopted various methods to tap this immortal source of powers. The methods are well known as japa, kirtan, fasting, pilgrimage, etc.

Concentration is the key to open the gates of that greatest power. When you successfully concentrate on one idea or form, you enter into dhyana. Whether you are a devotee of God or an atheist, you can realize the glory through meditation. A person having faith in God can meditate on any chosen form of God, through which he will realize him. An atheist also can be given a way to reach the destination. He can either meditate on a flower, or on a star, or on the tip of the nose, or between the eyebrows, or on the heart and so on. He can concentrate on nada according to the advice of an experienced master of nada yoga.

So long as you don't realize your real swarupa, you will continue to suffer from positive and negative charges of nature; you will not experience that supreme bliss, which is your personal property. This is your first and foremost duty.

Days are flying away. You have wasted so many years in vain. Whether you are a father, or a husband, you *can* walk upon this divine path. This path is not only accessible to a brahmin or a sannyasi. Every sincere soul can start on this pilgrimage to peace and power. Virtuous and saintly souls are ever ready to guide you at every step. The path of God is the only path. The glory of God is the only glory. All else is transitory and evanescent. Here is the way to maintain that divine happiness. Life is wastage without God-realization. Youth is a waste without yoga. Intellectual achievements are futile without meditation. Prosperity is a curse without peace. Manhood is a mockery without brahmacharya. In short, you are dead without that eternal life.

To sum up, meditation is a prerequisite for samadhi. Concentration precedes meditation as an essential step. Concentration presupposes name and form for its basis. Thus concentration culminates in meditation; meditation terminates in samadhi and self-realization. It is in this respect that you will have to look at yoga sadhana.

You may go to temples and discharge all religious obligations as taught by your tradition. But that alone will not help you to unlock the secret chambers. At best they will maintain a sense of fulfilment in your psychological condition. However much you may sit for puja, please note that lack of concentration will render all your efforts futile. It is always best to aim first and then shoot. There is practically no use shooting in the air. So understand that intense practice of concentration is quite essential. It is only then that real bliss will be experienced by you.

However, I don't discourage and demoralize your presupposed faith. You can repeat the name of your chosen deity in any way you like, anywhere you like and whenever you like. But do it with bhava, intense awareness and non-dual faith. Do it as you do your most important as well as serious work. Remember the name as you remember your beloved and newlywed wife. I don't stand in the way of your social and traditional beliefs. I merely suggest that you effect a reorientation.

Concentration is a faculty. This can be used in business, in the office, as well as elsewhere. Concentration helps in improving the personality of an individual. Concentration is a permanent aid to success in every sphere of life. Concentration paves a way to intuitional flashes of discovery in different fields of knowledge. It bestows keen insight and a ready reckoner intellectual capacity. It *somehow* acts as a potential medium to unearth occult treasures.

In the end, I wish to bring home to your mind that the right and proper way to the attainment of joy and happiness is to regain the lost eyesight by the practice of yoga sadhana. Awaken thy God from within. Wake up, O Shiva, from within,

110

from Kailash and dance on the bosom of thy mansarovar. I know you as my Shiva, my inner light, my Rama. Do thou descend upon thy children!

Pleasing others, swallowing the poison which someone gives to you, is no less than a divine trait, quite usual to Lord Shiva. Why then shouldn't we too live happily, easily and gladly in this life of various seasons.

One should continue the life of a householder so long as he is wanted there. If he wants to take to sannyasa, he must do sadhana. So long as he has not entered in the plane of God-consciousness, let him at least enjoy life in all its fullness. I don't know why we forget this; that we have come to experience the bliss, of which meditation is a higher form, and the world a finite expression. A dhobi's dogs live neither with their owner, nor at the river. They neither live happily in the world, nor control the mind by meditation. They neither do sadhana nor lead the fearless life of a householder.

The more one worries, the more one suffers. A boy worries about toys, a young man about women, a father about children, middle-aged men about fast-deteriorating health, old about young, and still older about the forthcoming pangs of death and hell. Still we are in search of happiness. O brother, in the babool tree one won't ever find mangoes.

Love is a divine force to annihilate worries. It is one of those heavenly drinks which frees man from the thraldom of dissatisfaction and spiritual unrest. Love, we have misunderstood it. Love does not demand. It is a dedication. Love knows nothing but sacrifice. Yes, at the altar of love I sacrificed my body, my soul, my all – all that I claimed to possess. 'Take it' is the real meaning of 'love'. 'Give me' is the watchword of an exploiter. Love does not exploit; love only enriches. Love is the only fertilizer of the soil of life.

111

Passion is not love. Greed is not love. Romance is not love. Attachment or attraction is not love. Love is an innermost feeling of the soul. Love is a state when our soul relaxes its tensions, when strains and burdens have been set aside, and the soul of man rests in the blissful lap of 'someone' divine. During meditation we can practise this love. When we are all alone, I mean really alone, we are with him. When this condition has materialized, do you think worries would still exist?

Delhi, December 24, 1958

Nobody should be allowed to renounce unless he has made remarkable progress in sadhana whilst amidst the congestion and responsibilities of life. A sadhaka of this world is far more perfect than a sadhu of an ashram. One can go to an ashram for some time, that is all. What exactly one needs is to expand the angle of vision and understanding. Wealth, wife and children are not at all the source of pain, neither is their absence the foundation of happiness. Real trouble exists in our attitude.

The mind acquires various experiences through the medium of the senses. Then it becomes powerful enough to overcome ourselves, more so when aided by passion. It is then that an advanced sadhaka also is affected by the tempest. Passion for the opposite sex is very hard to overcome. Then only come passions for wealth, name, fame, etc. Humanitarianism and devotion are sublimated forms of various designs of passion. Karma yoga is a sublimated form of expression of suppressed passions.

There is something else which can raise a sadhaka above this passion-mindedness. The safest measure to be adopted by such an aspirant who can't overcome passion is to get married and pacify the craving. Thus in the cycle of evolution, he might get a better chance of uninterrupted sadhana. Even while pacifying his innate passions in family

112

life, he can sincerely take to the practice of sadhana and make better progress than that man who has missed marriage and yet craves terribly for it.

Raipur (Rewa), January 10, 1959

The difficulty in meditation is this: that the inner mind does not grasp that object which it doesn't love. It can recall a flower of its choice more than it can think of a form which it doesn't relish.

Meditate on guru. This is the best way to materialize the form in the mind first, then in your consciousness where it will at once become a reality.

Stick to your guru mantra. That will give you all you pray for. Maha mantra and Maha Mrityunjaya and other mantras will form the basis for the prayer at the end of your upasana. Remember that the prayer is effective only if it is done while understanding its meaning. So you either follow the Sanskrit directly, or pray in the language you understand well. It is necessary for a sadhaka to know what he is praying for.

Guru mantra is only for repetition; and while repeating it, none else but the form should be in your mind. Prayer presupposes an attentive mind towards the object of your prayer. Japa is meant for awakening the spiritual power, while prayer is to direct that power for a particular and desired end. Hence, you can pray at the end of your japa, concentration and meditation.

Do your best, leave the rest. Spare no effort. Care not for success and failure. Take care of mental equilibrium. Remain as a sakshi. You are working as per his orders. He will give you necessary inspiration and provide you with suitable opportunities to render the divine work successful.

113

Do not meditate on two forms in any case. One, One and only One. There is no need thinking me in him and him in me. Straightforward meditation presupposes only one centre of upasana. Guru is the best. Feel one form of guru ever present in thee at all times. Don't confuse your mind by thinking Satyam is equal to God, and God is equal to guru. Are Baba, everything is the same.

The best object for meditation is one whom you love too much. It is not necessary that the beloved should be either God or guru. Even if it be a prostitute, you can surely acquire the faculty of single-mindedness thereby. Meditation is a state wherein the consciousness tries to express itself beyond any control.

Your path of sadhana must be plain, smooth and simple. Rama will not get angry if you do meditation on your guru only. Know that every form is his form; and each form, in its singleness, includes all forms. Visualize only one form. Repeat only one name. No delay. Guru is your centre of meditation; guru mantra the medium of japa. No fluctuation hereafter please. You will know, in the course of time, the need of a single form and a single name.

There is a great power under whose command we work and live. Let none of my disciples aim at the 'bread of blood'. Instead, let them enjoy contentment in the 'bread of milk'. I must strictly advise you to keep the temptations of maya away from you.

Satsang could be held underneath a tree, in a temple premises, in the house of anybody, or in no-man's land. This *was* and *is* a phase of your sadhana, which will be a barometer to test your mental fluctuations.

Even if nobody comes to satsang, sit alone and feel that the hall is full. Don't build castles in the mind. Mind is to be reserved for building his form and for a supramental flight.

You were inspired by him to undertake this work. The future will reveal unto you his purpose. You have not become

114

wise enough to follow his purpose. And so you go on; regularly go on. Truth alone triumphs.

Mind, body and pranas seem to be affected by each other; a disturbed condition in any of these three affects the rest. Keen sadhakas have felt this fact a great dissipating phenomenon.

It is really wonderful to note that the very same mind, striving for spiritual perfection, dives deep into those thoughts which counteract the progress of sadhana. The very same mind which resolves to stick to certain holy attitudes runs after unholy pursuits. Why this double dealing? Are there two different minds, or are its interests divided into two?

In fact, the mind is attracted by two different centres of gravity; namely, samskaras and sadhana. While satsang and an intense desire for realization pull it towards sadhana, the past experiences forcibly drag it into past reflections and future anticipations. Since already acquired perceptions have more intimacy with the mind, it grasps them far more easily, whereas matters relating to sadhana are almost strange to its knowledge, however much it might create interest in it.

When a sadhaka is rich with the samskaras of sadhana and when its practice forms a deep impression in his chitta, it is then that the centre of spiritual attraction becomes keener and mightier than the centre of samskaras.

The mind grows impatient if the object of concentration does not become vivid in thought consciousness. It slackens its usual zeal for concentration. One should continue with patience and perseverance.

Even during the process of concentration and afterwards, we feel that *someone* else in us was seeing the entire process. Surely it was other than the mind, because it seemed to be a witness of the mind also. What was it? Where was it; where is its seat in the body?

There is a stage *beyond waking* and *before sleeping*. It is not 'thinking' indeed. At this sharp point, when one is just crossing the field of sense consciousness and stepping into

115

causal consciousness, one is able to see as clearly as possible anything at random. He is visualizing a point, for example; he does it with as much success as we do when we are fully awake. So we draw a conclusion that even beyond jagriti one can see, hear and experience. You may call it anything. Let me call it self-consciousness with a lower 's'.

At this junction where unification of object of concentration takes place with the mind and its entire being, the sadhaka finds himself walking through the channel of sleep. This is the complaint with every sadhaka. Keen sadhakas detect this deviation, while the self-deluded take it for granted that this consciousness is samadhi. It is really a hard task to differentiate between these two phases of self, more so when one is in the field of concentration. Theoretically we know all about them. But then the difficulty comes in the practical field when a sadhaka at the verge of merger just slips into deep sleep or a state of mental suspension, only to find himself deviated when he regains sense consciousness. Very few sadhakas are endowed with a gift of control over their self-conscious perceptions.

Still fewer are they who can exert distinct discrimination at the juncture of full and overwhelming concentration, so as to avoid the departure for sleep consciousness, instead of self-consciousness.

It is here, at least, even a nirakara vadi sadhaka feels the need for a carved symbol or form, correctly speaking a humanized divine form in order to avoid total suspension of mind, which follows the unified condition of mind. A concrete form for concentration retains enough self-exerting consciousness in us to avoid total suspension or deep sleep. Mind continues to perceive the form even at the juncture of objective unconsciousness, which is exactly the point of departure towards unconsciousness.

Now objective awareness has dawned. Still the 'form awareness' clings to our thought. This is the way to self-consciousness wherefrom you can make a safe way to perfect meditation, resulting ultimately in samadhi. It is only here,

116

at the dawn of samadhi, that the form merges in formless-ness, by virtue of the emergence of superconsciousness. For it is a stage where not even a speck of mind functions. How then the form, or anything else? And this state of conscious-ness is to be experienced only by one's own self.

असतो मा सद्गमय।
तमसो मा ज्योतिर्गमय।
मृत्योर्माऽमृतं गमय।

सर्वेषां स्वस्तिर्भवतु।
सर्वेषां शान्तिर्भवतु।
सर्वेषां पूर्णं भवतु।
सर्वेषां मंगलं भवतु।

लोका: समस्ता: सुखिनो भवन्तु
सर्वे भवन्तु सुखिन: सर्वे सन्तु निरामया:
सर्वे भद्राणि पश्यन्तु मा कश्चिद् दु:खभाग्भवेत्

ॐ शांति: शांति: शांति:

From unreality lead me to reality!
From ignorance to enlightenment!
From mortality to immortality!

May good befall all!
May peace be unto all!
May all attain perfection!
May all reach auspiciousness!

May all worlds be happy!
May all be free from misery!
May all be free from disease!
May all experience bliss!
May none be unhappy!

Om Shanti Shanti Shanti!

117

Yoga Initiation Papers

YOGA INITIATION PAPER: ONE

1. Meditate daily on the 'faith culture':

1. An infinite power is in me, which I will realize.
2. I am God, the supreme power.
3. My guru and I are ONE. He is in me, I in him.
4. I don't worship numerous gods. I don't pray to anyone. I have in me the power of powers, which I will realize.
5. I am dedicated; I am devoted.
6. My thoughts can work miracles.
7. I have a miraculous power in me.
8. I am omnipotent, omniscient and omnipresent.
9. I have unshakeable faith that I am *that*; I will know this truth through intuition.
10. The day I transcend empirical consciousness by merging the mind in *me*, I will know *myself*.

2. The whole 'sadhana course' is in six steps:

(a) initiation, (b) concentration, (c) meditation, (d) re-initiation, (e) realization of atma shakti and (f) transcendental experiences.

3. Be guided by your resolutions:

1. I resolve to realize myself.
2. I resolve to be constantly aware of my guru, goal and mantra.
3. I resolve to meditate twice every day.
4. I resolve to practise asana and pranayama once every day.
5. I resolve to practise japa, prayers, introspection and self-analysis every day without fail.
6. I resolve not to be puffed up by the progress I make in sadhana.

121

7. I resolve to cultivate in myself divine virtues, viz., humility, love, service, forgiveness, forbearance, patience, perseverance, adaptability, etc., and to eradicate negative qualities, viz., anger, irritability, jealousy, narrow-mindedness, etc.
8. I resolve never to bow down to demi-gods and cemeteries and dead spirits.
9. I resolve never to exercise my willpower until I am re-initiated.
10. I resolve to be true and faithful to my sadhana, guru and myself.
11. I resolve not to waste a single minute in useless pursuits.
12. I resolve to live like a lotus in water, like a boat on a river, like the soft tongue in between two sets of sharp teeth.
13. I resolve to strive to fulfil my mission, while serving the society and family.
14. I resolve to give up non-vegetarian diet for good.
15. I resolve to give up visiting movies.
16. I resolve to study spiritual literature and attend religious congregations.
17. I resolve to avoid undesirable company, long discussions and obstinate conversations.
18. I resolve to be stronger still.
19. I resolve to keep this truth before me that whatever happens happens for the supreme good.
20. I resolve to refrain from criticism and ill-will.
21. I resolve to practise celibacy throughout my life.

4. Do not worry about the following:

(a) transmigration, (b) spiritualism, (c) ceremonies, (d) sin and merit, (e) gods, goddesses, spirits and evil forces.

5. Please be more particular about:

(a) love unto him, (b) dedication unto him, (c) faith in him, (d) power in yourself, (e) purity in yourself, (f) magnetism in yourself, (g) personal strength in yourself and (h) mental equilibrium.

6. You have to realize within you the following:

(a) the shakti, (b) the siddhis, (c) inseparability from him, (d) the way to *use* the spiritual power.

7. Please note in a nutshell: What is realization?

1. Perfect merger of mind in the meditational object.
2. Talking to him in meditation.
3. Receiving guidance and experience from him in meditation as regards samadhi.

8. A few of the symptoms of progress in spiritual life:

1. Objective experiences will not penetrate into the self.
2. The ideal of *upasana* will become clearer still.
3. You will become unaware of everything except the form of Ishta during that stage of meditation.
4. You will feel that the form has at once become conscious, living and moving.
5. Love will grow; passions will begin to subside.
6. Serenity will begin to prevail; hypersensitivity will be overcome.
7. You will never be disturbed either mentally or ethically.
8. A golden-yellow colour will begin to manifest around the form during deep meditation.
9. Sometimes you will materialize thoughts to your surprise.
10. Doubts will be cleared in meditation.
11. Whatever you say to the form will be communicated to your guru.
12. The person you think of will *at times* feel like coming to you.
13. The thing you desire will be *somehow* brought to you.
14. You will feel a peculiar lightness soon after you come out of meditation.
15. The speech will grow melodious and eyes lustrous and mind calm.
16. *At times* you will receive portents of future events, even without any intention on your part.
17. Those you come across will be drawn by your personality.

123

9. These are some of the cautions which you will have to keep in mind:

- Even if you have any knowledge of occult power developing in you, you should be *careful* that you don't exercise it, at any cost.
- Experiences of sadhana must be considered as 'top secret'.
- Desires for personal gain should be given up.
- Willpower should never be used *except* in the progress of sadhana.
- Don't look intently at anybody.
- Never indulge in palmistry, astrology and propitiation of various gods.
- Never believe in an unalterable destiny, or prarabdha.
- Don't discuss the topic of your sadhana before anyone who himself is not a sadhaka.
- Never meditate between 12 and 4 at night until you are re-initiated.
- Even if you have to attend rituals and spirit-ceremonies, do it without being in tune with them.
- Be prepared to discover the divine light and power unintimated.
- Don't fast and don't overload.
- Don't be receptive to criticism.
- Whatever others might say, you mind your own sadhana.
- Don't act or put on a show of being a sadhaka or a yogi. Weave around yourself a defensive wall, which will not allow others to know that you have the power and light. *Never, never and never* should you allow others to know about your sadhana and siddhi.
- Remain indifferent to praise and blame.
- Don't open a shop of 'blessings'.
- Use common sense at every step of yoga sadhana.
- Be aware that you are developing a great spiritual force within. *I repeat it once again*. 'Be aware that you are developing a great spiritual power within.'

10. Special instructions:

1. You need not do mantra writing if you feel like siting more for meditation.
2. If you cannot visualize your meditational object with closed eyes, then practise trataka with open eyes on the picture.
3. It is always good to keep a set of geru coloured clothes for sadhana.
4. Dinner must be taken by 8 p.m. at the latest. Delayed dinner interferes in meditation.
5. Practise meditation after yogasanas and pranayamas.
6. Don't discuss matters related to sadhana with obstinate persons.
7. There is no harm in shedding tears during prayers; but that should be done without being noticed.
8. Don't be particular about facial beauty.
9. Don't be lost in adverse conditions.
10. The main concern of a sadhaka is his sadhana. He who concerns himself with other matters is an extrovert. Such a sadhaka can't succeed in sadhana.
11. There will come a stage when you might get stray visions pertaining to your previous life. Unless the visions are thrust upon your mind forcibly, you should always take them to be serious impediments.
12. Don't analyze, recapitulate and believe in dreams or visions.
13. You are ceaselessly radiating 'thought currents' and receiving them as well. The only thing you are required to do is to realize this fact very well and believe in the potentiality of thoughts.

If you entertain sympathetic thoughts for somebody, you are emitting similar radiations which are received by his spirit, although his conscious mind is not aware of inner happenings.

If you have not trained your spirit, you will constantly receive various radiations even in deep sleep.

By the practice of sadhana, you create a defensive force against those incoming thought currents. At the same time, you contribute a high frequency to your own thoughts.

11. How to write a diary of spiritual progress:

A diary should tell a saga of spiritual effort. It should be a vehicle of the self. Not for artistic style, or display of one's experience by way of publication should one write a diary. We should write, if at all, from inner necessity.

Your diary must be a collection of inspiring auto-suggestions and ideas. Here is a sample:

"Even as butter is hidden in milk, likewise light and power are hidden within this body. I am light and power. I am not this body, not this mind, not these senses.

"Even when I am profoundly asleep, the experience of bliss and existence remains intact. This proves that in the absence of all sense activities also, the light and power remain unaffected.

"I am all-powerful. I am that infinite light which permeates everywhere. Sins don't contaminate me. Pains don't touch me. Injuries don't hurt me. A sword can't kill me. Water can't drench me. Fire can't burn me. I am an unchangeable and permanent wall upon which the changing scenes of the world come and go. I am *one* as well as *many*. I work through infinite hands. I eat through infinite mouths. I look out through infinite eyes. I am the life and protector of the infinite universe. I give light to the sun. I love all, for 'all' are nothing but 'my own self'.

"When I am in meditation, I feel that there is a magazine of infinite power in me. I am the knower of past, present and future. Within me is the microscopic film of ages and ages. I am beyond death and birth, beyond time, space and objects. I am infinite, immortal, bliss, wisdom and light."

This is a sample. It is this way that you will have to write your diary. Don't write about social problems. You can even express your feelings for your Lord. That will help you a lot. You can even describe various modes and shapes of your

126

beloved Lord. In short, anything concerning sadhana must be the items of your diary. Reading the diary will help you for meditation.

12. How to pray:

You should pray in all love, humility and confidence. The prayer mixed with emotion and feeling is at once heard and fulfilled. Don't simply utter Sanskrit slokas which you don't even understand. Pray unto him like a child. Remember any event of your life when your prayer was heard and fulfilled. Recollect that state of your mind.

Pray with perfect faith that he will listen to your prayer and fulfil it. Never pray for trifling things. Pray unto him for strength to face life. Pray for viveka, vairagya, love and service. Pray for purity of mind. Pray for meditation and celibacy. Pray unto him to come face to face and reveal knowledge unto you. Have faith that he is all-merciful and a kind father, and that he will give all you ask for. Pray to understand his merciful acts and loving blessings. Pray unto him for quick spiritual evolution. Pray unto him in all *love, faith* and *emotion*.

Now that all the preliminaries are over and you have been initiated into the order of yoga, Satyam wishes you a happy and absorbing spiritual career, and accepts you into his fold.

YOGA INITIATION PAPER: TWO

1. Message to the sadhaka:

In fact, the power is in you
what you need is confidence,
and a little practice.

Even now, you have that power,
though it lies unseen;
realize that power
through direct intuition.

Within you is the wisdom!
Dive deep, go in,
and you will realize the pearl!

If you concentrate and meditate,
you will see the truth actually.
That is siddhi!

Whenever you think,
think confidently;
be sure whatever you think
must come to pass.

You have to realize the highest,
minor siddhis cannot guide you;
hold this knowledge
to sustain your practices.

Let the form become abiding
and awareness perpetual,
then you will see the Light.

Form will become conscious;
this is the symptom of progress,
this is the key.

2. Twenty hints for an aspirant:

1. Self-realization is your goal.
2. Awareness of the goal will maintain your spirit for sadhana.
3. Be regular and punctual in meditation, asanas, pranayama, prayers and self-analysis.
4. Meditate in padmasana (or siddhasana).
5. Don't meditate when you are very tired. Avoid exertion.
6. Speak less. Stop loose thinking. Reduce your necessities.
7. During any physical illness, sumiran alone will do. No japa and no meditation; no asanas and pranayama.
8. Try to practise mental kirtan. No lip service. Merely imagine that the sound is being produced in the brain. Do only a little in the beginning.
9. When the sadhaka is sure that his spiritual zeal won't diminish, and that he can meditate 'without efforts' he should avoid intellectual big talk.
10. He should consider his 'aim, faith and success' alone as the first and last thing.
11. Like an arrow which has been let off, the sadhaka should have, strictly speaking, one way and one sadhana.
12. The sadhaka should not confuse himself with many aims under the garb of catholicity and broad-mindedness.
13. The sadhaka should be careful not to compile various ideas which come from different sources of philosophy and usher in intellectual chaos.
14. That sadhaka who consults books and forms his mental structure in accordance with the ideas contained in various books will find it really hard to achieve the power.
15. That sadhaka who has been properly initiated and instructed in the science of sadhana and yoga should have nothing to do with various scriptures, beliefs, orders and congregations.
16. The sadhaka should never change the course of his sadhana, never express it unto others, never analyze it intellectually.

17. That sadhaka who has been properly initiated and instructed in the science of sadhana and yoga shouldn't be emotionally moved by petty idols, temples and dualistic notions of reality. It is only after he has been established steadfastly in wisdom that he is free to act as he likes.

18. A sincere sadhaka, who is already in practice, should not have shastra vasana. It will destroy the tempo of his sadhana. It may even subdue his faith. In the course of time he reveals scriptural knowledge from within. He can discuss even without consulting any scripture. He can understand things by himself. He should patiently wait until intuition is awakened in him.

19. Even if there are hosts of defects, concentration will certainly overcome all of them. There is only one thing which should be entirely removed. That is the trait of jealousy. So long as one has jealousy in his heart, spiritual powers and meditational progress will do more harm than good. Siddhi, which is a direct result of self-purification, is really good and liberating. Therefore, understand that thorough purification is essential.

20. Fashion makes the vrittis extrovert and body-conscious. The sadhaka should remain contented with decency. One has to eliminate a certain type of fashion. Female sadhaka yogis should therefore keep their personalities free from emotional charges. They should neither receive nor emit vibrations of attraction and repulsion. The simpler the personality, the quicker the progress.

3. Aim, faith and success:
Adopt, decide and retain your aim throughout everything. Also, infuse and express faith sincerely. Constantly bear in mind that 'certainty about success leads to success'.

4. A few words about worldly success:
It goes without saying that everyone, in his inner core, wants worldly success even though he may outwardly appear

130

indifferent to it. He who has taken to yoga sadhana is bound to be successful in every field. He need not even wish to succeed. Then what? He has just to be sure and definite about his success in the work he has undertaken. He should 'relax his mind', while 'feeling sure' about his success. Indifference and relaxation coupled with definiteness and surety lead one to success.

A sadhaka can exert his will to bring about the desired success, but that might oppose nature at times, which is not at all desirable until he has followed the whimsical steps of nature and until he has developed in him 'a power', which can turn the steps of nature without causing any harm to anyone in the least.

Certain worldly success may prove to be a great obstacle in yoga sadhana. Therefore, it is always better to acquire knowledge of nature at first.

Surrender to guru or God is the easiest way to ensure mental equilibrium as well as worldly success. Therefore, I say again, "Simply resign to his will." This is the way, *the secret.*

However, there comes a time when the sadhaka has every right to bring his own full-fledged power into operation for the good of many. But that is possible only after re-initiation. Re-initiation is possible only:
1. After successful meditation.
2. After jealousy is burnt in toto.
3. After a few spiritual experiences during normal life or meditation.
4. After one has developed abundant altruism in oneself.

5. Grace of God and guru:

O sadhaka, if you want to attain the grace of God, *empty yourself of all worldly thoughts and take his name with every breath.* Surrender yourself unto him. Carry on the spiritual practices as instructed by your master with faith, love and sincerity. You will attain his grace.

6. Guru and disciple:

They are physically *two*. They will remain two. They are spiritually *one*. This will be just realized.

7. About the guru:

He has three aspects:
1. Physical body (perceived by the senses).
2. Mental radiation (received in sadhana).
3. Conscious form or chinmaya vigraha (seen in meditation only).

The physical body is seen only when one is awake. Mental radiations are felt during waking and sadhana. The conscious form is seen only during meditation.

8. About a disciple:

An advanced and receptive sadhaka is always in tune with the guru. Rather his mind thinks just the thoughts it receives from his guru. Successful sadhakas see the conscious form in meditation and get their doubts cleared, wisdom unearthed and the light revealed through the medium of that form of the guru.

9. Duration of sadhana:

(a) Love and sincerity, (b) clarity and faith, (c) practice and control alone decide the duration. You may merge in meditation at any moment. Be prepared.

10. After successful meditation:

If successful meditations are repeated day after day following the first merger, the sadhaka should temporarily withdraw himself completely from normal activities until the re-initiation has taken place.

If meditation culminates even once, one should withdraw oneself from normal activities just for a day or two until the first overwhelming has subsided. Even after the first culmination, meditation should be regularly continued for the remaining eleven days. The happiness at this stage is

132

beyond limit; normal consciousness is completely taken over by that limitless bliss. Hence this caution.

Re-initiation must follow within eleven days of the first successful combination. Better if earlier.

That sadhaka whose guru is no more alive should find another master of the same order for the purpose of re-initiation.

YOGA INITIATION PAPER: THREE

1. Thought communication:

My thoughts are reaching you; your thoughts are reaching me. Our inner consciousness is in tune with your thoughts. But since we haven't connected our outer consciousness with the inner one, we are unable to express or understand those radiations on our conscious plane.

Concentration and meditation will effect that desired connection between the outer mind and the inner mind. When that is over, you will simultaneously receive my thoughts on your conscious plane, as soon as they are received by the inner apparatus.

Whatever the mind thinks is of a refined quality. It is not gross. The ordinary mind is still not capable of converting those refined and subtle radiations into gross experiences.

During normal conditions, the mind is connected with the ten sense perceptions; but naturally it is disconnected from the inner consciousness, which is receiving constant thought radiations through its all-pervading sources.

Now we have to connect this consciousness with the *inner* one. This is possible only when the senses have been withdrawn towards *that* consciousness by any method.

No sooner are the sense perceptions introverted in concentration and meditation than the two faculties of the jiva get plugged into each other. Now the sense perceptions are merged into inner consciousness, and rendered subtle enough to conduct those thought radiations into the arena of the external mind.

Thus when the mind and senses are introverted towards the centre or inner consciousness, then the thought radiations (towards which the inner consciousness is ever receptive) are conducted towards the outer consciousness, or the mind.

134

When this is done, you naturally become capable of understanding, following and perceiving those radiations which I send on the plane of the indriyas, or through the gross external perceptions.

What your *inner consciousness* receives from me are subtle *radiations*, and what your *mind* is capable of thinking are *thoughts*. In order to transcribe radiations into thoughts, you have to reduce thoughts into a finer stuff by the practice of (a) withdrawal, (b) concentration, (c) meditation, and (d) samadhi.

Now that your mental thoughts have been converted into a form of *consciousness*, it has become capable of receiving, understanding and expressing those *radiations*.

When this is practised for a pretty long time, you will be able to undergo this process *at will*, even while you are outwardly conscious.

Of course, in the beginning those experiences are assimilated and understood, only to be forgotten during the wakening of sense consciousness. At a certain stage those experiences are remembered in the wakening of sense consciousness, like distant dreams.

When a sadhaka is blessed by his guru, he simultaneously receives and expresses those radiations or experiences even during the period of awakened sense consciousness, not to mention the experience in samadhi!

2. Phases of consciousness:

The mental condition at the wakening of sense perceptions may be termed as 'extrovert consciousness'.

The mental condition during the processes of concentration and meditation may be termed as 'introvert consciousness'.

The pure condition during samadhi may be termed as 'inner consciousness'.

These again may be termed as mind (thoughts), chitta (sensations) and jnana (knowledge) respectively; or in other words conscious, subconscious and superconscious.

135

3. What is extrovert consciousness?

The condition of mind, when experiences take place through the medium of the ten senses, the fourfold mind and the five pranas (nineteen in all) is to be known as extrovert consciousness. This consciousness is responsible for experiences in the waking condition. It hasn't got the capacity to be in tune with subtle thought radiations. It is technically termed bahir mukha vritti.

4. What is introvert consciousness?

The condition of mind when sense perceptions and mental activities are united in one thought current, and when the mind experiences irrespective of the presence of gross objects, is known as introvert consciousness. This state is materialized in true concentration and achieved fully in deep meditation. At that time it is not receptive to gross perceptions. It is a state wherein sensations are in full swing, and wherein there is but one idea, one form and one sound. It is technically known as antar mukha vritti.

5. What is inner consciousness?

The condition of mind when no sense perceptions, no mental sensations and no idea, name and form remain is known as the state of inner consciousness. At that time it is not in tune with gross sense perceptions. It is a state where suprasensual intuitive radiations, light and sound are experienced. This state is a direct culmination of dharana and dhyana. It is here that the knowledge dawns. This is also known as atma chetana.

6. Experiences in extrovert consciousness:

Seeing, hearing, tasting, touching and the rest of the ten kinds of experiences that you have during the waking condition; then again thinking, desiring and wishing as you experience them every day. The whole life is an expression of this extrovert consciousness.

136

7. Experiences in introvert consciousness:

In the beginning, there are distractions of course. You are aware of external perceptions also. Gradually the external objects diminish. The form of your Ishtam, his name or idea become clearer and clearer. There are scarce moments when you land in blankness as well. At times, there arises a strange feeling of ananda. At times you visualize lights of various colours. You also experience the form of your Ishtam, either glowing with a light, or getting fused into a flood of light. Then again you hear melodious, enlightening and unsounded Omkara. There are moments, when the surrounding space of your Ishtam is covered with numerous flowers of various colours.

At a certain stage, you might visualize men and women, places and things which you might have hitherto never seen or even thought of. This state is just a glimpse of your previous life. But such experiences are rare; usually one cannot remember them after returning to normal extrovert consciousness.

Various flowers of beauty, places of charm and men and women are seen. There are series of other experiences too.

There comes a stage when physical passions trouble and lower temptations try to assail. There is also a tendency to revolt against these practices.

8. Experiences in inner consciousness:

No more sensations. Only the form remains; and this *form* is in tune with that *inner consciousness*. Now this form becomes what I call *conscious form* or chinmaya vigraha. This stage is a culmination of faith, sincerity and love.

All other experiences cease; one forgets even oneself.

It is through the medium of this conscious form that everything is achieved. One is blessed by this conscious form. He is informed, cautioned and prompted about events in life. He is guided and given knowledge about the matters desired.

At first, the experiences of this stage are not at all remembered when one reverts to sense consciousness. But gradually these experiences become vivid even during the gross condition of the individual. If reminded by the guru, one can render them vivid even earlier.

At this stage, wisdom dawns, power is achieved and light perceived. This pure consciousness is God or atma, which was called jiva because of its tendencies to perceive externally. No sooner is it introverted than it shines in its original glory.

9. Centres of concentration:

(a) Central white spot of the left eye, (b) star within this spot, (c) space within the star and central white spot, (d) similarly regarding the right eye, (e) eyebrow centre, (f) left and right nostrils, (g) lips, and (h) the whole face.

10. Concentration on eyes:

1. Look at the right eye intently. It emits brilliant sunrays. Look at the left eye intently. It emits soothing moonlight. The right eye is the sun. The left is the moon.
2. The right eye-star is the sun. The left eye-star is the moon.
3. The white spot in the right eye-star is the centre of the sun. The white spot in the left eye-star is the centre of the moon.
4. The space behind and around the right eye-star is the sunlit sky. The space behind and around the left eye-star is the moonlit sky.
5. Concentrate on the right eye first, left next. Concentrate on each of the eyes to such an extent that nothing else except the point of concentration is seen within your vision.
6. Start concentration on the white centre of the right eye-star first. That is the bindu. That will not only become distinct, but will also begin to revolve. Ultimately you will see nothing but a white spot. This white spot is the centre of the sun.
7. Then come to the central spot of the other eye. Practise as per item 6.
8. Now come to the right eye-star until you see nothing but the star with a centre. Similarly, concentrate on the left also. The right is the sun, the left is the moon.

138

9. Now concentrate on the right space first, left space next, as sunlit and moonlit skies respectively.
10. When the concentration on the white centre of the star has become keen and really successful, then the next step becomes somewhat easier. You can more easily concentrate on the star. When this too has become successful, then the third step becomes still easier.

This much about the concentration on the eyes. If this concentration on the eyes becomes successful, the rest will become easier.

11. Eyebrows:

When the above has been accomplished, then concentrate on the eyebrow centre, *including* both the eyes also. This eyebrow centre is the seat of mystic energy, which gives light to both the sun and the moon (eyes). Imagine that the energy is flowing from the centre of the eyebrows towards both the eyes.

12. Nostrils:

When this too has been accomplished, then include the nose, and concentrate upon it. The two nostrils are twin rivers of 'consciousness vitale' or vital energy. Concentrate upon them as the inflowing rivers of the life force, which are known as ida and pingala or Ganga and Yamuna.

Concentrate on the right first, then on the left. Visualize that the twin rivers of vital energy are flowing in through them.

13. Lips:

Concentrate as it were upon four petals of a lotus dripping nectar drops. Nectar drops of inexplicable sweetness drip therefrom. They are also the seats of the divine smile. The colour is pink. They are four in number. Concentrate upon them as four lotus petals, pink in colour, sweet of smile and the seat of nectar drops.

14. Face:

Now you can visualize the whole face as the brahmanda, having over its round space the sun, moon, Ganga, Yamuna, central energy and lotus petals.

Surrounding the face, there is an aura, a beam of light.

This much for concentration with eyes open and with the picture present in front of you. Concentration, ideation and japa should go on simultaneously, sa vichara japa dhyana.

15. With closed eyes:

When it is quite dark and there is no light at all, then repeat the above processes serially on the mental screen, with eyes closed. Practise it gradually according to the sequence of concentration as mentioned previously. Ultimately visualize the whole face.

Note: If of course you can visualize the whole face without any effort, then you need not go into these rituals.

And if you have developed your own process of concentration, then also you need not go into these rituals.

16. Conclusion:

When all the processes are complete, then the whole face will become distinct on the mental screen. You can see it surrounded by a glow of astral light.

Although the whole form is also good for sumiran, still the clear conception of the face alone should be considered as a prerequisite. When the face has become distinct on the mental plane, then you can conceive the whole form at will. If you find the full form coming easily and automatically, no harm; go on.

Since the face is the centre of power, we aim at making the face as real as reality itself. The face is the seat of light, power, blessing, wisdom and beauty. It is an expression of atma. When it has been rendered clear in meditation, all results are achieved. The face is an emblem of purity, serenity, love and attraction.

YOGA INITIATION PAPER: FOUR

The mind is like an ocean. Thoughts are like waves arising therefrom. Your duty is to calm down these thoughts by japa, concentration and meditation on your Ishtam. Concentration will lead you to meditation where there is only one thought of Ishtam. Faith, self-control, awareness, intense practice, surrender and absence of experienced sensations of all types enhance the success in concentration.

It is essential that the meditational object (dhyeya) is one, constant and lovely. You should remember it well that you really believe in the divinity of your Ishtam.

No thought should interfere with rupa sadhana and nama sadhana. The entire attention is to be concentrated on japa and dhyana. When this is practised unceasingly, then the real steadiness comes. You should neither lose courage, nor should you be unpunctual.

Attraction towards painful and pleasuresome experiences should be abandoned in toto. Every work is to be done by the body, indriyas and the routine mental mechanism. Every perception is to be limited to indriyas and manas alone. When one dissolves one's atma from the mind and indriyas, he attains real vairagya. Vairagya is not physical inactivity, nor is it absent-mindedness. It is just a topsy-turvy change in one's own attitude towards repulsive and attractive experiences and their bases. Just remain a witness. Then see, work and think.

Normal duties need neither be minimized nor stopped. They do not come in the picture at all. When the atma is separated, then actions and mental workings do not bind the sadhaka. When the sadhaka brings in the bhava of instrumentality, his mind is not at all affected. It is for *him* and at *his* will and pleasure that the sadhaka should consider

141

himself working, thinking and seeing. Thus he will be able to maintain himself even while working, thinking and seeing. Thus he will be able to maintain normal interest, intelligence and efficiency. What one needs in cultivating vairagya is to consider oneself working at his orders and remain ever balanced in thought, word and actions.

This type of vairagya is essential in order to strengthen the powers of sadhana. This is the only way for a man to work for his spiritual enlightenment.

Physical illness, slavery to the senses and mental disturbances form the *first* obstacle.

Losing interest in sadhana is the *second* obstacle.

Carelessness and hurry-burry in sadhana is the *third* obstacle.

Heaviness in body and mind due to sleep and lethargy is the *fourth* obstacle.

Attraction towards and awareness of enjoyments and sense experiences form the *fifth* obstacle.

Considering one's own method of sadhana as improper is the *sixth* obstacle.

Unattainment of even elementary progress after a long term of sadhana is the *seventh* obstacle.

Instability of mind in any stage of sadhana is the *eighth* obstacle.

Apart from these few obstacles, there are those factors which one should know as impediments, disturbing the peace and bliss of one's mind. The greatest among the obstacles is to consider one's present condition as unfavourable, one's own progress as doubtful, one's own sadhana as defective, one's own life as hellish, and one's own normal avocation as opposed to his spiritual progress.

One should really realize that his meditational object is not merely a photograph, but a platform for the descent of the divine. He should understand throughout everything that the more he concentrates on the picture, the clearer his Ishtam will become. Let it become a truth of his mind that his Ishtam is everywhere, even though he is encased in a body for the favour of his bhaktas. The first and the last truth is that he should constantly be aware of this fact; that there is every truth in this saying: *"He will appear before thee in flesh and blood, reveal unto thee jnana and converse with thee."*

When all vrittis pertaining to external experiences have subsided, and when one single vritti is prevailing throughout everything, then the sadhaka attains the pure stage of meditation. And when this stage of single vritti alone continues, and when no other thought or vritti is felt in the least, then one is said to have attained samprajnata samadhi. When the entire consciousness of the sadhaka is transformed into the form of the Ishtam to the extent that he is seen as clearly as anything, the ever-glowing darshan is known as samprajnata samadhi.

In the first stage, the form is seen as you see the picture. It means that you are still conscious of the external world. As soon as the awareness becomes single, and the feeling of love reaches its highest stage, and *no other than the beloved* is remembered, then the Ishtam, the immortal form of Ishtam, manifests before you as truly as you would like him to be. In fact, all this takes place in the state of wholesale merger and non-dual awareness. The form is the same whom you know, but so far you have not seen him on account of sensual and mental limitations. Now that you have reached that stage where your atma has become all-pervading because of the absence of sensual and mental limitations, you are able to see him.

As soon as the form is apprehended, he enters in the form. He is in front of you in that familiar swarupa you meditated upon. He is conscious, yet he sits or stands quietly. You keep on looking at him and he at you. This takes time. When you have looked at him for some time, emotions bubble forth, tears flow and mechanically you fall down at his feet.

The sadhaka should see *that* form continuously for not less than seven days. On the following day of manifestation also he should sit for meditation as usual. But instead of meditating on the photo, he should bring into his mind the

143

scene of manifestation and thus awaken his awareness. This process should be continued so long as the deity doesn't come to you at any place instantaneously. If you are able to see him at any time you *will*; then you should start conversing with him, and praying unto him. You can also repeat the mantra along with him.

No sooner will you sit for meditation at this stage than you see him in his usual posture in front of you. You look at him and he at you. Suddenly you break into emotions and bow down at his feet. He blesses and disappears. Now you come down to physical consciousness and faintly remember the experience as if it were a distant dream. Joy and ananda become boundless. Mind becomes calm, quiet and serene. The power of magnetism grows intense. The voice grows sweet. Your prayers are fulfilled and your questions answered. Beware that you do not exploit this achievement for personal and petty ends.

And there comes a stage where the lower self is completely transformed and the mental screens (fluctuations) are torn. Pure atma bhava dawns. The sadhaka becomes a siddha-master of his mind, senses and body. Knowledge emerges spontaneously. Revelation after revelation. He becomes powerful, full of wisdom, a kalpa vriksha, and a fit receptacle for Brahma anubhava, which is his final goal.

GLOSSARY

Abhyasa – constant uninterrupted practice

Adwaita anubhuti – experience of non-dual consciousness

Ahamkara – sense of I-ness; ego; centre of individual physical, mental and psychic functioning

Ajapa japa – spontaneous repetition of mantra

Ajnana – absence of knowledge; ignorance

Alasya – procrastination; laziness

Anadi – eternal; having no beginning

Ananda – undying felicity or bliss

Anasakti – detachment

Antar mukha vritti – introverted tendency

Anubhava – knowledge derived through intimate, personal experience

Anushthana – performance or accomplishment of an act; a resolve to perform sadhana with absolute discipline for a required period of time

Aparoksha jnana – knowledge gained through the medium of the senses

Apnapan – a sense of belonging

Arati – waving lights before a deity with reverence

Are baba – 'hey father'

Are bhai – 'hey brother'

Asana – traditionally a comfortable meditative pose for inducing steadiness; a specific position of the body for channelling prana

Ashanti – disturbed state of mind

Ashram – a place of spiritual retreat and inner growth through internal and external labour

Asthira manas – the fluctuating and wavering mind

Atma – pure awareness; soul or inner spirit; the universal atma (paramatma) manifests as the individual atma (jivatma)

145

Atma anubhuti – experience of the inner self or atma

Atma bhava – attitude of spiritual awareness

Atma chetana – self-awareness

Atma chintan – self-introspection

Atma eva idam sarvam – the consciousness is manifested in everything

Atma maya – the illusory force of the self or pure consciousness, responsible for the creation of matter

Atma shakti – spiritual force of energy

Atma smaran – remembrance of the inner self

Avidya – ignorance

Babool – a thorny tree

Baccha – child

Badrinath – a place of pilgrimage dedicated to Lord Vishnu, situated in the Himalayas

Bahir mukha vritti – extroverted tendency

Bahoorupiye – one who assumes many forms; multi-faceted man

Bhagavad aradhana – worship of the divine

Bhajan – devotional song

Bhakta – devotee

Bhakti – intense inner devotion or love

Bhastrika – bellows breathing technique for increasing and purifying energy or prana

Bhava – inner attitude or feeling

Bhavana – development by means of thought; meditation

Bhrama – illusion or erroneous perception

Bhu loka – terrestrial plane of existence

Bhuvar loka – intermediate realm between heaven and earth

Bilwamangal – previous name of saint Tulsidas

Bindu – nucleus, source of creation

Brahma – one aspect of the Hindu trinity of divinity; creator of the universe

Brahma anubhava – personal experience of the supreme self

Brahmacharya – celibacy; redirection of sexual energy through yogic practices for spiritual experience

Brahman – supreme self

146

Brahmanda – cosmos

Brahmanishta – one who is established in the experience of Brahman or non-dual awareness

Brahmashrotriya – one who is well-versed in the subject of the supreme reality

Brahma Vidya gurus – enlightened teachers with experience of Brahma

Buddhi – intellect; also creative intelligence

Chaitanya – one of the great saints of Bengal who advocated bhakti yoga

Chakkar baji – futile acts, running around in circles

Chalta phirta Rama – seeing divinity in different forms

Chandra nadi – ida nadi or flow of mental energy

Chinmaya vigraha – consolidated form of consciousness

Chinta – worries

Chintamani – wish-fulfilling gem; also the name of the wife of Bilwamangal

Chitta – inner faculty of individual consciousness; storehouse of samskaras or archetypes

Conch – shell blown like a trumpet as a rallying call, used in puja or exoteric worship

Crore – ten million

Daharakasa – space within the heart cavity

Darshan – to see; spiritual vision; to have inner vision or blessing of the divine power

Dayananda – a reformer saint who lived in India in the 19th century founder of the Arya Samaj movement

Devas – literally means 'illumined ones'; higher forces or powers

Devata – lord, or one who is illumined

Dharma – duty; code of harmonious living; righteous path or act

Dhobi – person who washes clothes for a living

Dhun – melody

Dhyana – meditation; stage of introversion and concentration of mind in which the meditator and object of meditation come within close range of each other

Dhyeya – purpose

Dukha – pain, frustration, misery

Dwesha – aversion, dislike

Ekanta – alone, by oneself, solitude

Ek-rupa – a single form

Ganga – river Ganges, the longest and most sacred river in India; correlates with ida nadi

Gautam Buddha – the illumined one; an enlightened sage who lived in India approximately 2,500 years ago, after whom Buddhism originated

Gaya – a place of pilgrimage in India

Ghat – funeral pyre

Gita – song; short for Bhagavad Gita, 'Song of God', one of the best loved and most practical scriptures explaining the twelve types of yoga; part of the historical epic Mahabharata

Gopis – milkmaids; devotees of Krishna

Govinda – name of Krishna

Grihastha – householder

Gunas – qualities; the threefold aspects of prakriti or nature which are present in every form of creation; see sattwa, rajas and tamas, saguna and nirguna

Guru – dispeller of darkness; spiritually enlightened soul who by the grace of his own atma can dispel darkness, ignorance and illusion from the mind of a disciple

Guru Poornima – the first full moon day in the month of July when devotees pay homage to their guru and the guru meditates on behalf of all disciples

Halasana – plough pose

Hamsa – swan

Hatha – 'ha' signifies sun, 'tha' signifies moon, indicating the two forces of energy in the physical body responsible for all mental and vital functions

Hatha yoga – a system of yoga specifically dealing with the practices of bodily purification, in which the two forces of energy existing in the physical body are brought into harmony by a systematic series of practices, such as asana, pranayama, mudra, bandha and shatkarma

Ida nadi – major pranic/psychic channel in the subtle body which conducts mental energy throughout the body and mind, located on the left side of the body; the 'tha' of hatha yoga, indicates the moon or lunar force

Indriya anubhuti – sense experience or awareness

Indriyas – sense organs of cognition and action, ten in number; see jnanendriyas and karmendriyas

Ishavasya Upanishad – Ishavasya literally means 'enveloped by God'; an Upanishad concerned with the supreme knowledge of divine immanence and all-pervasiveness

Ishta devata – tutelary deity; one's personal symbol; form or vision of divinity

Ishwara – Lord, God; pure consciousness

Jada samadhi – root; fully established samadhi; solid state; unflinching

Jagriti – conscious realm; material world of the senses

Jagte raho – 'stay awake'

Jala neti – nasal cleansing technique using warm salty water

Jana loka – plane of seers and sages

Japa – conscious and continual repetition of mantra

Japa sahita dhyana – state of meditation which is attained through the continual repetition of mantra

Jiva – individual soul

Jivanmukta – term used for a soul who is liberated while living

Jnana – wisdom

Jnanendriyas – sense organs of knowledge, five in number: (ears, eyes, nose, tongue and skin)

Kaikeyi – one of the wives of King Dasharatha in the great epic Ramayana; mother of Bharata, stepmother of Rama.

Kailash – holy mountain in Tibet

Kailash mansarovar – abode of Shiva, considered to be the cosmic centre of the universe; lake at the foot of Mount Kailash

Kalpa taru – mythological concept of a wish-fulfilling tree

Kalpa vriksha – divine tree

Kama – passion

Kapalbhati – breathing technique for purifying frontal lobes of the brain

149

Karana sharira – causal body

Karma – action; law of cause and effect; the sum total of man's destiny which determines the course of his life

Karmendriyas – organs of action, five in number: hands, feet, larynx, excretory organs, reproductive organs

Kedarnath – a place of pilgrimage dedicated to Lord Shiva, situated in the Himalayas

Khud garzi – self-pleasing

Kirtan – devotional song composed of mantras

Kripa – grace; kindness; blessing

Krishna – eighth incarnation of Lord Vishnu, the cosmic sustainer; the principal figure of the Bhagavad Gita

Ksheer sagar – limitless ocean

Kshetra – field

Kshetragyar – chief of that area

Kumbhaka – breath retention

Lagan – physical or mental unity; total immersion in thought, word and deed

Laya – stage of dissolution of mind where separation of body and consciousness is experienced

Lila – divine play; cosmic game of consciousness and energy

Loka – world; dimension or plane of existence or consciousness, seven in number; see bhu, bhuvar, maha, swar, tapo, jano and satya lokas

Maha loka – plane of saints and siddhas

Maha mantra – the great mantra; the mantra 'Hare Rama, Hare Krishna' is known as the maha mantra due to its universality

Maha mrityunjaya – mantra used for combating disease or death

Mala – rosary made from tulsi, sandalwood, rudraksha or crystal, used as an aid in japa and meditation

Mamata – maternal love; attachment

Manas – mind; inner faculty which creates sankalpa/vikalpa, thought/counterthought

Man bahalav – recreation of the mind

Mandir – temple

Manasarovar – literally means the lake of the mind; see Kailash mansarovar

Mansoor – Sufi saint

Mantra – particular subtle sound vibration capable of liberating the energy and consciousness from matter

Marga – path

Marga bandhu – friend on this path

Math – religious institution

Maya – illusory force responsible for erroneous perception in man; the cause of the phenomenal world

Mayurasana – peacock pose

Merji – wish

Mira – female saint born in the early 16th century in Rajasthan, India; a great devotee of Lord Krishna

Moha – confusion

Moksha – liberation from the cycle of birth, death and rebirth

Mouna – vow of silence

Mridanga – a large drum made of clay, used as a musical accompaniment in India

Nada – subtle sound vibration; inner sound

Nada anusandhana – discovery of the subtle inner sound

Nadi – river; flow; psychic channel for the distribution of prana in the subtle body

Nama – name; divine name

Nama japa – repetition of the divine name

Nama sadhana – spiritual practice involving repetition of the divine name

Nama sankirtan – chanting the divine name

Nama sumiran – remembrance of the divine name

Narayana – the sustainer of the cosmos

Nirakara – formless reality

Nirakara vadi – one who believes in the formless reality

Nirguna – beyond the three gunas; devoid of any qualities or limitations

Nirvana – enlightenment; samadhi; harmony between the individual consciousness and universal consciousness

Nirvikalpa samadhi – samadhi without even subjective patterns of the mind

Nishkama bhakti – devotion without expectation

Nivritti – retirement; cessation; return; see pravritti

Nivritti marga – attainment of self-realization through the path of non-involvement or renunciation

Om – cosmic vibration of the universe; universal mantra. (same as Aum); represents four states of mind: conscious, subconscious, unconscious and supraconscious or cosmic mind

Omkara – the syllable of Om

Om Nama Shivaya – mantra dedicated to Lord Shiva

Padmasana – lotus pose; basic meditative pose in which one sits with the right foot resting on the left thigh and the left foot resting on the right thigh

Param – supreme; highest

Paramatma – universal atma

Param hamsa – supreme swan; title bestowed on one who is able to distinguish between reality and unreality, truth and untruth, consciousness and matter

Parloka – the other world

Paschimottanasana – the back stretching pose

Pingala nadi – major pranic/psychic channel in the subtle body which conducts the vital energy throughout the body and mind, located on the right side of the body; the 'tha' of hatha yoga, indicates the sun or solar force

Prajna – intuition; revelation

Prakriti – nature; manifest creation

Pramad – procrastination

Prana - life force; vital energy permeating and sustaining life and creation, both in the micro and macro cosmos

Pranayama – yogic practices of manipulating and controlling the flow of prana in the subtle body, by control of the respiratory process

Prarabdha – deep karmic influences; one of three types of karma to which the jiva is subjected

Pratyahara – sense withdrawal

Pravritti – involvement; activity; functioning; see nivritti

Pravritti marga – attainment of self-realization through the path of total involvement

Prem – love

Pukka – solid

Puja – worship

Pujarin – worshipper; temple priest

Purusha – pure consciousness; male principle; see prakriti

Radha – foremost devotee of Lord Krishna

Raga – attachment; one of the five afflictions according to Patanjali

Rajas – one of the three qualities of prakriti representing the dynamic, active state of mind and nature

Rakhi – a ceremonial thread that a sister ties on her brother's wrist as a symbol of her love and his acceptance to protect her from the adversities of life

Rama – divine name; often used as a mantra

Rasa – the blissful essence of love

Rasagulla – delicious Indian sweet made from milk and sugar

Ravana – demon king in the great epic Ramayana

Roti – a yeastless flat bread made in India

Rupa – form

Rupa sadhana – spiritual practice involving concentration on a form

Saag – green leafy vegetable

Sadhaka – one who practises sadhana

Sadhana – spiritual practice done regularly for attainment of inner experience and realization of self, true reality and cosmic consciousness

Sadhu – a holy person

Saguna – within the realm of the three gunas; manifest state of higher reality, attributed with form and qualities

Sahasrara – the highest evolutionary centre in man situated at the top of the head, containing all the chakras within itself; thousand-petalled

Sakama – worship performed with expectation of reward

Sakara – with form

Samadhi – the fulfilment of meditation; supraconscious state of union between the object of meditation and the universal consciousness

Samprajnata samadhi – samadhi experience with some kind of basis, content, centre, symbol or seed; culminates in seedless samadhi; see nirvikalpa samadhi

Samskara – latent mental impression stored in the subtle body and subconscious mind as an archetype

Sankalpa – spiritual resolve; willpower; also thought

Sannyasa – spiritual surrender; an order of renunciation

Sarai – an inn

Sat-chit-ananda – truth-consciousness-bliss

Satsang – literally 'in the company of truth'; meeting with spiritually minded people

Sattwa – one of the three qualities of prakriti representing an equilibrated state of mind and nature

Satya loka – plane of truth and reality

Satyam – truth

Sa vichar japa – a meditation on mantra, not devoid of vikalpa or thought patterns

Seths – rich businessmen

Shakti – kinetic principle of consciousness; vital energy force; female aspect of Shiva or consciousness

Shanti – peace, inner serenity

Sharan – refuge

Shastra – authoritative treatise on any subject, particularly science and religion

Shastra adhyayan – practice and learning of the scriptures

Shastra vasana – knowledge for the sake of knowledge

Shavasana – corpse pose; a posture for relaxation

Sheetali – cooling breath; breathing technique in which the tongue is extended and rolled into a tube through which air is inhaled

Sheetkari – hissing breath; breathing technique utilized in pranayama in which air is noisily inhaled through the clenched teeth

Shishya – student; disciple; one willing to learn

Shiva – one aspect of the Hindu trinity of divinity; destroyer of the universe; pure consciousness; male counterpart of Shakti

Shivoham – I am Shiva

Shuddha – pure

Siddha – one who is perfected; adept who has developed his psychic and pranic capacity and power

Siddhi – perfection; activated pranic and psychic capacity

Sirshasana – headstand pose

Smaran – remembrance

Sri Sukadeva – a saint enlightened from birth; one on the maha siddhas

Sukha – happiness, pleasure

Sukhasana – comfortable cross-legged sitting posture

Sukshma drishta – subtle inner vision

Sumiran – one-pointed spiritual awareness; remembrance of mantra or divine name

Surdas – 19th century poet and saint of India

Surya nadi – pingala nadi or flow of vital energy

Surya namaskara – 'salute to the sun'; revitalizing sequence of postures related to the twelve signs of the zodiac

Sushupti – unconscious realm and state of mind; deep sleep; third state of consciousness according to yoga philosophy

Swabhava – behaviour and nature

Swadhyaya – self-study, self-reflection; study of the scriptures

Swapna – dream state related to the subconscious mind; the second state of consciousness according to yoga philosophy

Swar loka – heaven; divine plane of existence

Swarupa – form

Tamas – one of the three qualities of prakriti representing the dull, inert state of mind and nature

Tamasha – spectacle; sideshow

Tanmaya – complete involvement

Tapa loka – plane of liberated souls

Tattwa – essential element or principle; literally means 'thatness'

Tirtha – holy place of pilgrimage

Trataka – practice of steadily gazing at or concentrating on an external or internal object or centre

Turiya – supraconscious state beyond the realm of the gunas; the unmanifest state of pure consciousness; the fourth state of consciousness according to yoga philosophy

Turiyateeta – transcendental consciousness

Tyaga – abandonment; renunciation

Upadesha – instruction; verbal command

Upanishad – literally means 'to sit close by'; part of the Vedas; there are traditionally 108 Upanishads containing dialogues between guru and disciple on the nature, reality and identity of the individual and cosmic consciousness

Upasana – worship; concentration

Vairagya – supreme dispassion; non-attachment; state in which one is internally calm and tranquil amidst the tumultuous events of the world

Vajrasana – thunderbolt pose

Vasanas – latent, or deep seated desires

Vedas – the oldest written texts revealed to the sages and saints in India, expressing knowledge of the whole universe; four in number, divided into Samhita, Brahmana, Aranyaka and Upanishad

Veena – stringed musical instrument

Vidya – internal experience; knowledge; spiritual light

Vishayananda – sense pleasure

Vishnu – one aspect of the Hindu divine trinity; the sustainer of the universe

Vishwatman – universal soul

Viveka – discrimination

Vritti – a modification arising in the mind and consciousness due to samskaras or archetypes; likened to the circular wave pattern emanating when a stone is dropped into a still pool of water

Vyakta – manifest

Vyavaharic – practical

Yaad – remembrance

Yamuna – sacred river in India, correlates with pingala nadi

Yoga – union; a systematic science of the body and mind leading to the union of the individual consciousness with the universal or cosmic consciousness

156

SYNOPSIS OF THE LIFE OF
SWAMI SATYANANDA SARASWATI

Swami Satyananda Saraswati was born in 1923 at Almora (Uttaranchal) into a family of farmers. His ancestors were warriors and many of his kith and kin down the line, including his father, served in the army and police force.

However, it became evident that Sri Swamiji had a different bent of mind, as he began to have spiritual experiences at the age of six, when his awareness spontaneously left the body and he saw himself lying motionless on the floor. Many saints and sadhus blessed him and reassured his parents that he had a very developed awareness. This experience of disembodied awareness continued, which led him to many saints of that time such as Anandamayi Ma. Sri Swamiji also met a tantric bhairavi, Sukhman Giri, who gave him shaktipat and directed him to find a guru in order to stabilize his spiritual experiences.

In 1943, at the age of 20, he renounced his home and went in search of a guru. This search ultimately led him to Swami Sivananda Saraswati at Rishikesh, who initiated him into the Dashnam Order of Sannyasa on 12th September 1947 on the banks of the Ganges and gave him the name Swami Satyananda Saraswati.

In those early years at Rishikesh, Sri Swamiji immersed himself in guru seva. At that time the ashram was still in its infancy and even the basic amenities such as buildings and toilets were absent. The forests surrounding the small ashram were infested with snakes, scorpions, mosquitoes, monkeys and even tigers. The ashram work too was heavy and hard, requiring Sri Swamiji to toil like a labourer carrying bucket loads of water from the Ganga up to the ashram and digging canals from the high mountain streams down to the ashram many kilometres away in order to store water for constructing the ashram.

Rishikesh was then a small town and all the ashram requirements had to be brought by foot from far away. In addition there were varied duties, including the daily pooja at Vishwanath

Mandir, for which Sri Swamiji would go into the dense forests to collect bael leaves. If anyone fell sick there was no medical care and no one to attend to them. All the sannyasins had to go out for bhiksha or alms as the ashram did not have a mess or kitchen.

Of that glorious time when he lived and served his guru, Sri Swamiji says that it was a period of total communion and surrender to the guru tattwa, whereby he felt that just to hear, speak or see Swami Sivananda was yoga. But most of all his guru's words rang true, for through this dedication and spirit of nishkama seva he gained an enlightened understanding of the secrets of spiritual life and became an authority on Yoga, Tantra, Vedanta, Samkhya and kundalini yoga. Swami Sivananda said of Swami Satyananda, "Few would exhibit such intense vairagya at such an early age. Swami Satyananda is full of Nachiketa vairagya."

Although he had a photographic memory and a keen intellect, and his guru described him as a versatile genius, Swami Satyananda's learning did not come from books and study in the ashram. His knowledge unfolded from within through his untiring seva as well as his abiding faith and love for Swami Sivananda, who told him, "Work hard and you will be purified. You do not have to search for the light, the light will unfold from within you."

In 1956, after spending twelve years in guru seva, Swami Satyananda set out as a wanderer (parivrajaka). Before his departure Swami Sivananda taught him kriya yoga and gave him the mission to "spread yoga from door to door and shore to shore".

As a wandering sannyasin, Swami Satyananda travelled extensively by foot, car, train and sometimes even by camel throughout India, Afghanistan, Burma, Nepal, Tibet, Ceylon and the entire Asian subcontinent. During his sojourns, he met people from all stratas of society and began formulating his ideas on how to spread the yogic techniques. Although his formal education and spiritual tradition was that of Vedanta, the task of disseminating yoga became his movement.

His mission unfolded before him in 1956 when he founded the International Yoga Fellowship Movement with the aim of creating a global fraternity of yoga. Because his mission was revealed to him at Munger, Bihar, he established the Bihar School of Yoga in Munger. Before long his teachings were rapidly spreading throughout the world. From 1963 to 1983, Swami Satyananda took yoga to each and every corner of the world, to people of every caste, creed, religion and nationality. He guided millions of seekers in all continents and established centres and ashrams in different countries.

His frequent travels took him to Australia, New Zealand, Japan, China, the Philippines, Hong Kong, Malaysia, Thailand, Singapore, USA, England, Ireland, France, Italy, Germany, Switzerland, Denmark, Sweden, Yugoslavia, Poland, Hungary, Bulgaria, Slovenia, Russia, Czechoslovakia, Greece, Saudi Arabia, Kuwait, Bahrain, Dubai, Iraq, Iran, Pakistan, Afghanistan, Colombia, Brazil, Uruguay, Chile, Argentina, Santo Domingo, Puerto Rico, Sudan, Egypt, Nairobi, Ghana, Mauritius, Alaska and Iceland. One can easily say that Sri Swamiji hoisted the flag of yoga in every nook and cranny of the world.

Nowhere did he face opposition, resistance or criticism. His way was unique. Well-versed in all religions and scriptures, he incorporated their wisdom with such a natural flair that people of all faiths were drawn to him. His teaching was not just confined to yoga but covered the wisdom of many millenniums.

Sri Swamiji brought to light the knowledge of Tantra, the mother of all philosophies, the sublime truths of Vedanta, the Upanishads and Puranas, Buddhism, Jainism, Sikhism, Zoroastrianism, Islam and Christianity, including modern scientific analysis of matter and creation. He interpreted, explained and gave precise, accurate and systematic explanations of the ancient systems of Tantra and Yoga, revealing practices hitherto unknown.

It can be said that Sri Swamiji was a pioneer in the field of yoga because his presentation had a novelty and freshness. Ajapa japa, antar mouna, pawanmuktasana, kriya yoga and prana vidya are just some of the practices which he introduced in such a methodical and simple manner that it became possible for everyone to delve into this valuable and hitherto inaccessible science for their physical, mental, emotional and spiritual development.

Yoga nidra was Sri Swamiji's interpretation of the tantric system of nyasa. With his deep insight into this knowledge, he was able to realize the potential of this practice of nyasa in a manner which gave it a practical utility for each and every individual, rather than just remaining a prerequisite for worship. Yoga nidra is but one example of his acumen and penetrating insight into the ancient systems.

Sri Swamiji's outlook was inspiring, uplifting as well as in-depth and penetrating. Yet his language and explanations were always simple and easy to comprehend. During this period he authored over eighty books on yoga and tantra which, due to their authenticity, are accepted as textbooks in schools and universities throughout the world. These books have been translated into Italian, German, Spanish, Russian, Yugoslavian, Chinese, French, Greek, Iranian and most other prominent languages of the world.

People took to his ideas and spiritual seekers of all faiths and nationalities flocked to him. He initiated thousands into mantra and sannyasa, sowing in them the seed to live the divine life. He exhibited tremendous zeal and energy in spreading the light of yoga, and in the short span of twenty years Sri Swamiji fulfilled the mandate of his guru.

By 1983, Bihar School of Yoga was well established and recognized throughout the world as a reputed and authentic centre for learning yoga and the spiritual sciences. More than that, yoga had moved out of the caves of hermits and ascetics into the mainstream of society. Whether in hospitals, jails, schools, colleges, business houses, the sporting and fashion arenas, the army or navy, yoga was in demand. Professionals such as lawyers, engineers, doctors, business magnates and professors were incorporating yoga into their lives. So too were the masses. Yoga had become a household word.

Now, at the peak of his accomplishment, having fulfilled his guru's wish, Swami Satyananda renounced all that he created and appointed his successor, Swami Niranjanananda, to continue the work.

In 1988 Sri Swamiji renounced disciples, establishments and institutions, and departed from Munger, never to return again, on a pilgrimage through the siddha teerthas of India, as a mendicant, without any personal belongings or assistance from the ashrams or institutions he had founded.

At Trayambakeshwar, the jyotir linga of Lord Mrityunjaya, his ishta devata, he renounced his garb and lived as an avadhoota, during which time his future place of abode and sadhana were revealed to him.

According to the mandate of his ishta devata, which was revealed to him at the source of the Godavari river near Neel Parbat at Trayambakeshwar (Maharashtra), Swami Satyananda came to the cremation ground of Sati in 1989, and took up residence in Rikhia, on the outskirts of Baba Baidyanath Dham in Deoghar (Jharkhand).

Swami Satyananda has been residing at Rikhia since September 1989. During this period he has undertaken long and arduous sadhanas such as Panchagni and Ashtottar-shat-laksh (108 lakh) mantra purascharana. Here he entered the lifestyle of the Paramahamsas who do not work for their flock and mission alone but have a universal vision. He does not associate with any institutions, nor does he give diksha, upadesh or receive dakshina, but remains in seclusion and sadhana, only on rare occasions coming out to give darshan to devotees who are always yearning for a glimpse of him.

INTERNATIONAL YOGA FELLOWSHIP MOVEMENT (IYFM)

The IYFM is a charitable and philosophical movement founded by Swami Satyananda at Rajnandgaon in 1956 to disseminate the yogic tradition throughout the world. It forms the medium to convey the teachings of Swami Satyananda through its affiliated centres around the world. Swami Niranjanananda is the first Paramacharya of the International Yoga Fellowship Movement.

The IYFM provides guidance, systematized yoga training programs and sets teaching standards for all the affiliated yoga teachers, centres and ashrams. A Yoga Charter to consolidate and unify the humanitarian efforts of all sannyasin disciples, yoga teachers, spiritual seekers and well-wishers was introduced during the World Yoga Convention in 1993. Affiliation to this Yoga Charter enables the person to become a messenger of goodwill and peace in the world, through active involvement in various far-reaching yoga-related projects.

BIHAR SCHOOL OF YOGA (BSY)

The Bihar School of Yoga is a charitable and educational institution founded by Swami Satyananda at Munger in 1963, with the aim of imparting yogic training to all nationalities and to provide a focal point for a mass return to the ancient science of yoga. The Chief Patron of Bihar School of Yoga is Swami Niranjanananda. The original school, Sivanandashram, is the centre for the Munger locality. Ganga Darshan, the new school established in 1981, is situated on a historic hill with panoramic views of the river Ganges.

Yoga Health Management, Teacher Training, Sadhana, Kriya Yoga and other specialized courses are held throughout the year. BSY is also renowned for its sannyasa training and the initiation of female and foreign sannyasins.

BSY provides trained sannyasins and teachers for conducting yoga conventions, seminars and lectures tours around the world. It also contains a comprehensive research library and scientific research centre.

SIVANANDA MATH (SM)

Sivananda Math is a social and charitable institution founded by Swami Satyananda at Munger in 1984, in memory of his guru, Swami Sivananda Saraswati of Rishikesh. The Head Office is now situated at Rikhia in Deoghar district, Jharkhand. Swami Niranjanananda is the Chief Patron.

Sivananda Math aims to facilitate the growth of the weaker and underprivileged sections of society, especially rural communities. Its activities include: distribution of free scholarships, clothing, farm animals and food, the digging of tube-wells and construction of houses for the needy, assistance to farmers in ploughing and watering their fields. The Rikhia complex also houses a satellite dish system for providing global information to the villagers.

A medical clinic has been established for the provision of medical treatment, advice and education. Veterinary services are also provided. All services are provided free and universally to everyone, regardless of caste and creed.

YOGA RESEARCH FOUNDATION (YRF)

The Yoga Research Foundation is a scientific, research-oriented institution founded by Swami Satyananda at Munger in 1984. Swami Niranjanananda is the Chief Patron of the foundation.

YRF aims to provide an accurate assessment of the practices of different branches of yoga within a scientific framework, and to establish yoga as an essential science for the development of mankind. At present the foundation is working on projects in the areas of fundamental research and clinical research. It is also studying the effects of yoga on proficiency improvement in various social projects, e.g. army, prisoners, children. These projects are being carried out in affiliated centres worldwide.

YRF's future plans include literary, scriptural, medical and scientific investigations into other little-known aspects of yoga for physical health, mental well-being and spiritual upliftment.

SRI PANCHDASHNAM PARAMAHAMSA ALAKH BARA

SRI PANCHDASHNAM PARAMAHAMSA ALAKH BARA
(PPAB)

Sri Panchdashnam Paramahamsa Alakh Bara was established in 1990 by Swami Satyananda at Rikhia, Deoghar, Jharkhand. It is a charitable, educational and non-profit making institution aiming to uphold and propagate the highest tradition of sannyasa, namely vairagya (dispassion), tyaga (renunciation) and tapasya (austerity). It propounds the tapovan style of living adopted by the rishis and munis of the vedic era and is intended only for sannyasins, renunciates, ascetics, tapasvis and paramahamsas. The Alakh Bara does not conduct any activities such as yoga teaching or preaching of any religion or religious concepts. The guidelines set down for the Alakh Bara are based on the classical vedic tradition of sadhana, tapasya and swadhyaya, or atma chintan.

Swami Satyananda, who resides permanently at the Alakh Bara, has performed the Panchagni Vidya and other vedic sadhanas, thus paving the way for future paramahamsas to uphold their tradition.

बिहार योग भारती
BIHAR YOGA BHARATI

BIHAR YOGA BHARATI (BYB)

Bihar Yoga Bharati was founded by Swami Niranjanananda in 1994 as an educational and charitable institution for advanced studies in yogic sciences. It is the culmination of the vision of Swami Sivananda and Swami Satyananda. BYB is the world's first accredited institution wholly devoted to teaching yoga. A comprehensive yogic education is imparted with provision to grant certificates and diplomas in yogic studies. It offers a complete scientific and yogic education according to the needs of today, through the areas of Yoga Philosophy, Yoga Psychology, Applied Yogic Science and Yogic Ecology.

Residential courses of four months to one year are conducted in a gurukul environment, so that along with yoga education, the spirit of seva (selfless service), samarpan (dedication) and karuna (compassion) for humankind is also imbibed by the students.

YOGA PUBLICATIONS TRUST (YPT)

Yoga Publications Trust (YPT) was established by Swami Niranjan-ananda in 2000. It is an organization devoted to the dissemination and promotion of yogic and allied knowledge – psychology (ancient and modern), ecology, medicine, vedic, upanishadic, tantric darshanas, philosophies (Eastern and Western), mysticism and spirituality – nationally and internationally through the distribution of books, magazines, audio and video cassettes and multimedia.

YPT is primarily concerned with publishing textbooks in the areas of yoga philosophy, psychology and applied yogic science, research materials, practice texts and the inspiring talks of eminent spiritual personalities and authors aimed at the upliftment of humanity by means of the eternal yogic knowledge, lifestyle and practice.